The Ideal Muslimah

Ibn Kathir

Content

Books by Ibn Kathir & Ibn Al-Qayyim

* Stories of the Prophets

 ISBN 9781643543888

* Seerah of Prophet Muhammad

 ISBN 9781094860213

* Stories of the Koran

 ISBN 9781095900796

* The Path to Guidance

 ISBN 9781643540818

* Purification of the Soul – Vol 1

 ISBN 9781643541389

* Tafseer Ibn Kathir

 ISBN 9781512266573

* Al-Fawaid: Wise Sayings

 ISBN 9781727812718

* Heaven's Door

 ISBN 9781643541396

* Soul's Journey after Death

  ISBN 9781643541365

* Koran: English Easy to Read

  ISBN 9781643540924

* Characteristics of Hypocrites

  ISBN 9781643541358

* Diseases of the Hearts

  and their Cures

  ISBN 9781643541129

* Timeless Seeds of Advice:

  (Don't Be Sad)

  ISBN 9798784227515

* The Holy Quran – Clear and

Easy to Read: in English

  ISBN 979851591373

<u>Introduction</u>

"Wasting time is worse than death, because death separates you from this world whereas wasting time separates you from Allah."

All praise is due to Allāh alone, we praise Him, we seek His love, aid and His forgiveness. We seek refuge in Allāh alone from all the evils of our souls and the evils of our deeds and actions. Whomsoever Allāh guides then there is none to misguide and whomsoever Allāh misguides then there is none to guide ever. I bear witness that there is none worthy of worship except Allāh, the Creator of All Things. He has no partners and I bear witness that Muhammad (peace be upon him) is His servant and last messenger. O you have believed, be pious to Allah with His true piety, and definitely do not die except as Muslims. (3:102)

يَٰٓأَيُّهَا ٱلَّذِينَ ءَامَنُوا۟ ٱتَّقُوا۟ ٱللَّهَ حَقَّ تُقَاتِهِۦ وَلَا تَمُوتُنَّ إِلَّا وَأَنتُم مُّسْلِمُونَ ﴿١٠٢﴾

This book contains verses from the Qur'an, sayings of the Prophet Muhammad (Peace and blessings be upon him) and of his Companions as well as of the wise. This book is not limited to Muslims, for any non-Muslim who reads it with an open mind will appreciate the author's ideas and thoughts, ideas that are based on the firm footing of revealed texts and thoughts. The author took into consideration feelings and emotions that are common to everyone. Nevertheless, the author wrote it based on the true Religion (whether we deviate from it or not) that is intrinsic to us all.

When you wake up in the morning, do not expect to see the evening, so live as though today is your last day. Yesterday has passed with its good and evil, however tomorrow has not yet arrived. If you find yourself to be in a very difficult or distress situation, show kindness to others, and you will be the first to find solace and comfort. Give to the needy, defend the oppressed, help those in distress, and visit the sick: you will find that happiness surrounds you from all directions.

An act of charity is like perfume because it will benefit everyone that is near - the user, the seller, and the buyer. O mankind, fear your Lord, who created you from one soul and created from it its mate and dispersed from both of them many men and women. And fear Allah, through whom you ask one another, and the wombs. Indeed Allah is ever, over you, an Observer.

يَـٰٓأَيُّهَا ٱلنَّاسُ ٱتَّقُوا۟ رَبَّكُمُ ٱلَّذِى خَلَقَكُم مِّن نَّفْسٍ وَٰحِدَةٍ وَخَلَقَ مِنْهَا زَوْجَهَا وَبَثَّ مِنْهُمَا رِجَالًا كَثِيرًا وَنِسَآءً وَٱتَّقُوا۟ ٱللَّهَ ٱلَّذِى تَسَآءَلُونَ بِهِۦ وَٱلْأَرْحَامَ إِنَّ ٱللَّهَ كَانَ عَلَيْكُمْ رَقِيبًا ﴿١﴾

Blessed is He in whose hand is dominion, and He is over all things competent. He who created death and life to test you as to which of you is best in deed - and He is the Exalted in Might, the Forgiving. (67:1-2)

تَبَـٰرَكَ ٱلَّذِى بِيَدِهِ ٱلْمُلْكُ وَهُوَ عَلَىٰ كُلِّ شَىْءٍ قَدِيرٌ ﴿١﴾

ٱلَّذِى خَلَقَ ٱلْمَوْتَ وَٱلْحَيَوٰةَ لِيَبْلُوَكُمْ أَيُّكُمْ أَحْسَنُ عَمَلًا وَهُوَ ٱلْعَزِيزُ
ٱلْغَفُورُ ۝ ٢

And they ask you (O Muhammad) concerning
the Ruh (the Spirit); Say: "The Ruh (the Spirit):
it is one of the things, the knowledge of which
is only with my Lord. And of knowledge, you
(mankind) have been given only a little."
(17:85)

وَيَسْـَٔلُونَكَ عَنِ ٱلرُّوحِ قُلِ ٱلرُّوحُ مِنْ أَمْرِ رَبِّى وَمَآ أُوتِيتُم مِّنَ
ٱلْعِلْمِ إِلَّا قَلِيلًا ۝ ٨٥

O People of the Scripture, do not commit
excess in your religion or say about Allāh
except the truth. The Messiah, Jesus, the son of
Mary, was but a messenger of Allāh and His
word which He directed to Mary and a soul
[created at a command] from Him. So believe
in Allāh and His prophets and messengers.
And do not say, Three; desist-it is better for
you. Indeed, Allāh is but one God. Exalted is
He above having a son.

To Allāh belongs whatever is in the heavens and whatever is on the earth. And sufficient is Allāh as Disposer of affairs.

يَٰٓأَهْلَ ٱلْكِتَٰبِ لَا تَغْلُوا۟ فِى دِينِكُمْ وَلَا تَقُولُوا۟ عَلَى ٱللَّهِ إِلَّا ٱلْحَقَّ إِنَّمَا ٱلْمَسِيحُ عِيسَى ٱبْنُ مَرْيَمَ رَسُولُ ٱللَّهِ وَكَلِمَتُهُۥٓ أَلْقَىٰهَآ إِلَىٰ مَرْيَمَ وَرُوحٌ مِّنْهُ فَـَٔامِنُوا۟ بِٱللَّهِ وَرُسُلِهِۦ وَلَا تَقُولُوا۟ ثَلَٰثَةٌ ٱنتَهُوا۟ خَيْرًا لَّكُمْ إِنَّمَا ٱللَّهُ إِلَٰهٌ وَٰحِدٌ سُبْحَٰنَهُۥٓ أَن يَكُونَ لَهُۥ وَلَدٌ لَّهُۥ مَا فِى ٱلسَّمَٰوَٰتِ وَمَا فِى ٱلْأَرْضِ وَكَفَىٰ بِٱللَّهِ وَكِيلًا ﴿١٧١﴾

Those Messengers! We preferred some to others; to some of them Allāh spoke (directly); others He raised to degrees (of honor); and to Isa (Jesus), the son of Maryam (Mary), We gave clear proofs and evidences, and supported him with Ruh-ul-Qudus [Jibrael (Gabriel)]. If Allāh had willed, succeeding generations would not have fought against each other, after clear Verses of Allāh had come to them, but they differed-some of them believed and others disbelieved.

If Allāh had willed, they would not have fought against one another, but Allāh does what He likes.

بِسْمِ اللّٰهِ الرَّحْمٰنِ الرَّحِيْمِ

تِلْكَ الرُّسُلُ فَضَّلْنَا بَعْضَهُمْ عَلَىٰ بَعْضٍ مِّنْهُم مَّن كَلَّمَ اللَّهُ وَرَفَعَ بَعْضَهُمْ دَرَجَٰتٍ وَءَاتَيْنَا عِيسَى ابْنَ مَرْيَمَ الْبَيِّنَٰتِ وَأَيَّدْنَٰهُ بِرُوحِ الْقُدُسِ وَلَوْ شَآءَ اللَّهُ مَا اقْتَتَلَ الَّذِينَ مِنۢ بَعْدِهِم مِّنۢ بَعْدِ مَا جَآءَتْهُمُ الْبَيِّنَٰتُ وَلَٰكِنِ اخْتَلَفُوا فَمِنْهُم مَّنْ ءَامَنَ وَمِنْهُم مَّن كَفَرَ وَلَوْ شَآءَ اللَّهُ مَا اقْتَتَلُوا وَلَٰكِنَّ اللَّهَ يَفْعَلُ مَا يُرِيدُ ﴿٢٥٣﴾

Allah promises the believing men and believing women gardens beneath which rivers flow, wherein they abide eternally, and pleasant dwellings in gardens of perpetual residence; but approval from Allah is greater. It is that which is the great attainment. (9:72)

وَعَدَ اللَّهُ الْمُؤْمِنِينَ وَالْمُؤْمِنَٰتِ جَنَّٰتٍ تَجْرِى مِن تَحْتِهَا الْأَنْهَٰرُ خَٰلِدِينَ فِيهَا وَمَسَٰكِنَ طَيِّبَةً فِى جَنَّٰتِ عَدْنٍ وَرِضْوَٰنٌ مِّنَ اللَّهِ أَكْبَرُ ذَٰلِكَ هُوَ الْفَوْزُ الْعَظِيمُ ﴿٧٢﴾

Iman (inward faith in Allāh)

"Women are one half of society which gives birth to the other half so it is as if they are the entire society."

One of the most important attributes of a good woman, is her deep faith in Allāh (God), and her sincere conviction that whatever happens in this earthly life, and whatever fate befalls her, only happens through the will and decree of Allāh; whatever befalls her would have been impossible to avoid, and whatever does not happen cannot be made to happen without Allāh's permission.

The hijrah to Allah includes abandoning what He hates and doing what He loves and accepts. Whoever works righteousness, woman or man, and has Faith, verily, to him will We give a new Life, a life that is good and pure and We will bestow on such their reward according to the best of their actions. (16:97)

مَنْ عَمِلَ صَلِحًا مِّن ذَكَرٍ أَوْ أُنثَىٰ وَهُوَ مُؤْمِنٌ فَلَنُحْيِيَنَّهُۥ

حَيَوٰةً طَيِّبَةً وَلَنَجْزِيَنَّهُمْ أَجْرَهُم بِأَحْسَنِ مَا كَانُوا۟

يَعْمَلُونَ ۝ (٩٧)

Allāh hath promised the Hypocrites men
and women, and the rejecters, of Faith, the
fire of Hell: Therein shall they dwell: Sufficient
is it for them: for them is the curse of Allāh,
and an enduring punishment. (9:68)

وَعَدَ ٱللَّهُ ٱلْمُنَٰفِقِينَ وَٱلْمُنَٰفِقَٰتِ وَٱلْكُفَّارَ نَارَ جَهَنَّمَ

خَٰلِدِينَ فِيهَا هِىَ حَسْبُهُمْ وَلَعَنَهُمُ ٱللَّهُ وَلَهُمْ عَذَابٌ

مُّقِيمٌ ۝ (٦٨)

Humans have no choice in this life but to strive towards the Righteous Path and to do good deeds. Like acts of prayer and worship, by whatever means one can, putting all our trust in God, submitting to His will, and believing that we always in need Allah's help and support. Contrary to what some believe, Allāh does not prohibit women from going out to fulfill their needs. However, God lays down a proper code of behavior, which is primarily intended to safeguard the modesty, dignity and honor of men and women. On that day you will see the faithful men and the faithful women -- their light running before them and on their right hand-- good news for you today: gardens beneath which rivers flow, to abide therein, that is the grand achievement. (57:12)

يَوۡمَ تَرَى ٱلۡمُؤۡمِنِينَ وَٱلۡمُؤۡمِنَٰتِ يَسۡعَىٰ نُورُهُم بَيۡنَ أَيۡدِيهِمۡ وَبِأَيۡمَٰنِهِم بُشۡرَىٰكُمُ ٱلۡيَوۡمَ جَنَّٰتٌ تَجۡرِى مِن تَحۡتِهَا ٱلۡأَنۡهَٰرُ خَٰلِدِينَ فِيهَا ذَٰلِكَ هُوَ ٱلۡفَوۡزُ ٱلۡعَظِيمُ ﴿١٢﴾

"O my Lord! Forgive me, my parents, all who enter my house in Faith, and (all) believing men and believing women: and to the wrong-doers grant Thou no increase but in perdition! (71:28)

رَبِّ اغْفِرْ لِي وَلِوَالِدَيَّ وَلِمَن دَخَلَ بَيْتِيَ مُؤْمِنًا وَلِلْمُؤْمِنِينَ وَالْمُؤْمِنَاتِ وَلَا تَزِدِ الظَّالِمِينَ إِلَّا تَبَارًا ۝

The perfection of Tawheed is found when there remains nothing in the heart except Allāh. Allāh, the Creator of humans, knows our nature better than anyone, and thus Allah has prescribed appropriate rules of behavior and appearance to be observed when men and women interact with one another in a social milieu. These rules of interaction also include a prescription for modesty in dress, talk and walk, etc.

1. Lowering the gaze: Indeed it is the most precious ornament of a woman is modesty, and the best expression of modesty is in the lowering of the gaze, as Almighty Allāh says, [...And tell the believing women that they should lower their gazes...] (An-Nur 24: 31)

وَقُل لِّلْمُؤْمِنَٰتِ يَغْضُضْنَ مِنْ أَبْصَٰرِهِنَّ وَيَحْفَظْنَ فُرُوجَهُنَّ وَلَا يُبْدِينَ زِينَتَهُنَّ إِلَّا مَا ظَهَرَ مِنْهَا وَلْيَضْرِبْنَ بِخُمُرِهِنَّ عَلَىٰ جُيُوبِهِنَّ وَلَا يُبْدِينَ زِينَتَهُنَّ إِلَّا لِبُعُولَتِهِنَّ أَوْ ءَابَآئِهِنَّ أَوْ ءَابَآءِ بُعُولَتِهِنَّ أَوْ أَبْنَآئِهِنَّ أَوْ أَبْنَآءِ بُعُولَتِهِنَّ أَوْ إِخْوَٰنِهِنَّ أَوْ بَنِىٓ إِخْوَٰنِهِنَّ أَوْ بَنِىٓ أَخَوَٰتِهِنَّ أَوْ نِسَآئِهِنَّ أَوْ مَا مَلَكَتْ أَيْمَٰنُهُنَّ أَوِ ٱلتَّٰبِعِينَ غَيْرِ أُو۟لِى ٱلْإِرْبَةِ مِنَ ٱلرِّجَالِ أَوِ ٱلطِّفْلِ ٱلَّذِينَ لَمْ يَظْهَرُوا۟ عَلَىٰ عَوْرَٰتِ ٱلنِّسَآءِ وَلَا يَضْرِبْنَ بِأَرْجُلِهِنَّ لِيُعْلَمَ مَا يُخْفِينَ مِن زِينَتِهِنَّ وَتُوبُوٓا۟ إِلَى ٱللَّهِ جَمِيعًا أَيُّهَ ٱلْمُؤْمِنُونَ لَعَلَّكُمْ تُفْلِحُونَ ۝٣١

2. Not intermingling with any men in such a way that their bodies come in contact or that a man touches women, as happens so often happens at the market. It is better for one of you to be pricked in the head with an iron pick than to touch a woman whom it is unlawful to touch. Tell the believing men to lower their gaze (from looking at forbidden things), and protect their private parts (from illegal sexual acts, etc.). That is purer for them. Verily, Allāh is All-Aware of what they do. (24:30)

قُل لِّلْمُؤْمِنِينَ يَغُضُّوا مِنْ أَبْصَـٰرِهِمْ وَيَحْفَظُوا فُرُوجَهُمْ ذَٰلِكَ أَزْكَىٰ لَهُمْ إِنَّ ٱللَّهَ خَبِيرُۢ بِمَا يَصْنَعُونَ ﴿٣٠﴾

3. Her clothing must conform to the standards laid down by Allah:

a) Her dress must cover her entire body with the exception of [that which is apparent] (An-Nur 24:31) which, refers to the face and hands.

b) It must never be transparent, revealing what is underneath it. The Prophet (peace and blessings be upon him) has informed us that, "Among the dwellers of hell are such women as are clothed yet naked, seducing and being seduced.

These shall not enter the Beautiful Garden, nor shall (even) its fragrance reach them. "Here, the meaning of "clothed yet naked" is that their light, thin, transparent garments do not conceal what is underneath.

c) Her dress must not be too tight so as to define the parts of her beautiful body, especially its curves, even though it may not be transparent.

This describes many of the styles of clothing current our current world. Women who wear such clothes likewise fall under the definition of "clothed but naked", since such a dress is often more provocative than one which is transparent.

d) She should never wear clothes which are specifically for men, such as trousers. If a heart becomes attached to anything other than Allah, Allah makes him dependent on what he is attached to. And he will be betrayed by it. Allah's Prophet (peace and blessings be upon him) was very sad when he saw women trying to resemble men and men trying to resemble women. He prohibited women from wearing men's clothing and vice-versa.

e) In her choice of clothing, a woman should try not to imitate others, for Islam disapproves of conformity to non-Islamic modes and desires its men and women to develop their own distinctive characteristics in appearance, as well as in beliefs and excellent attitudes.

Allah's Prophet (peace and blessings be upon him) said: "Whoever imitates a people is one of them. The heart will rest and feel relief if it is settled with Allah. And it will worry and feel anxious if it is settled with the people."

And as for women past child-bearing who do not expect wed-lock, it is no sin on them if they discard their (outer) clothing in such a way as not to show their adornment.

But to refrain (i.e. not to discard their outer clothing) is better for them. And Allāh is All-Hearer, All-Knower. (24:60)

وَالْقَوَاعِدُ مِنَ النِّسَاءِ الَّتِي لَا يَرْجُونَ نِكَاحًا فَلَيْسَ عَلَيْهِنَّ جُنَاحٌ أَن يَضَعْنَ ثِيَابَهُنَّ غَيْرَ مُتَبَرِّجَاتٍ بِزِينَةٍ وَأَن يَسْتَعْفِفْنَ خَيْرٌ لَّهُنَّ وَاللَّهُ سَمِيعٌ عَلِيمٌ ﴿٦٠﴾

4. Sins have many side-effects. One of them
   is that they steal knowledge from you. A
   woman that loves Allāh must walk and
   talk in a dignified and business-like
   manner, avoiding flirtatiousness in her
   facial expressions and movements.
   Please remember that flirting and
   seductive behavior are characteristics of
   wrong-minded women, not of Muslims.

Allāh said: [Then do not be too pleasant of
speech, lest one in whose heart there is a
disease should feel desire (for you) ...] (Al-
Ahzab 33:32)

يَٰنِسَآءَ ٱلنَّبِيِّ لَسْتُنَّ كَأَحَدٍ مِّنَ ٱلنِّسَآءِ إِنِ ٱتَّقَيْتُنَّ فَلَا تَخْضَعْنَ
بِٱلْقَوْلِ فَيَطْمَعَ ٱلَّذِي فِي قَلْبِهِۦ مَرَضٌ وَقُلْنَ قَوْلًا مَّعْرُوفًا ﴿٣٣﴾

If the heart becomes hardened, the eyes become dry. Tell the believing women to lower their gaze (from looking at forbidden things), and protect their private parts (from illegal sexual acts, etc.) and not to show off their adornment except only that which is apparent (like palms of hands or one eye or both eyes for necessity to see the way, or outer dress like veil, gloves, head-cover, apron, etc.), and to draw their veils all over Juyubihinna (i.e. their bodies, faces, necks and bosoms, etc.) and not to reveal their adornment except to their husbands, their fathers, their husband's fathers, their sons, their husband's sons, their brothers or their brother's sons, or their sister's sons, or their (Muslim) women (i.e. their sisters in Islam), or the (female) slaves whom their right hands possess, or old male servants who lack vigor, or small children who have no sense of the shame of sex. And let them not stamp their feet so as to reveal what they hide of their adornment. And all of you beg Allāh to forgive you all, O believers, that you may be successful.

Beware of every hour and how it passes, and only spend it in the best possible way, do not neglect yourself or Allah, but render it accustomed to the noblest and best of actions, and send to your grave that which will please you when you arrive to it. This worldly life is like a shadow. If you try to catch it, you will never be able to do so. If you turn your back towards it, it has no choice but to follow you.

Love of Allah is the power of the heart, the sustenance of the heart, the light of the heart. When Allah tests you it is never to destroy you. And when He removes something in your possession it is only in order to empty your hands for an even greater gift. Whoever desires to purify their heart, then let them prefer Allah to their desires. There is no joy for the one who does not bear sadness, there is no sweetness for the one who does not have patience, there is no delight for the one who does not suffer, and there is no relaxation for the one who does not endure fatigue.

5. A woman's tongue and actions can give you the taste of her heart. A woman that loves Allāh does not draw men's attention to her concealed adornment by the use of perfume or by jingling or toying with her ornaments or other such things. Many such women in the time of jahiliyyah (before the Prophet was sent) used to stamp their feet like donkeys when they passed by men so that the jingling of their ankle-bracelets might be heard.

Allāh forbade this, both because it might tempt a weak man to pursue her and also because it demonstrates the evil intention of the woman in attempting to draw the attention of men to herself. Allāh said: [They should not strike their feet in order to make known what they hide of their adornment...] be sincere in your actions and you will find the support of Allah surrounding you. The keys to the life of the heart lie in reflecting upon the Quran, being humble before Allah in secret, and leaving sins.

O Prophet! When believing women come to
you to give you the Bai'a (pledge), that they will
not associate anything in worship with Allāh,
that they will not steal, that they will not
commit illegal sexual intercourse, that they will
not kill their children, that they will not utter
slander, intentionally forging falsehood (i.e. by
making illegal children belonging to their
husbands), and that they will not disobey you
in any Ma'ruf (Islamic Monotheism and all that
which Islam ordains) then accept their Bai'a
(pledge), and ask Allāh to forgive them, Verily,
Allāh is Oft-Forgiving, Most Merciful.

يَٰٓأَيُّهَا ٱلنَّبِيُّ إِذَا جَآءَكَ ٱلْمُؤْمِنَٰتُ يُبَايِعْنَكَ عَلَىٰٓ أَن لَّا يُشْرِكْنَ بِٱللَّهِ
شَيْـًٔا وَلَا يَسْرِقْنَ وَلَا يَزْنِينَ وَلَا يَقْتُلْنَ أَوْلَٰدَهُنَّ وَلَا يَأْتِينَ بِبُهْتَٰنٍ
يَفْتَرِينَهُۥ بَيْنَ أَيْدِيهِنَّ وَأَرْجُلِهِنَّ وَلَا يَعْصِينَكَ فِى مَعْرُوفٍ
فَبَايِعْهُنَّ وَٱسْتَغْفِرْ لَهُنَّ ٱللَّهَ إِنَّ ٱللَّهَ غَفُورٌ رَّحِيمٌ ﴿١٢﴾

The Prophet's (peace be upon him) said: "The woman who perfumes herself and passes through a gathering is an adulteress. Any woman who perfumes herself and passes by a group of people so that her scent reaches them is an adulteress."

Allāh does not require, as many people claim, that a woman must remain confined to her house until death takes her out to her grave. On the contrary, a woman may go out for prayer, for her studies, and for her other lawful needs, both religious and secular, as was customary among the women of the families of the Companions and the women of later generations. Moreover, this early period, during the Prophet's time, we consider to be the best and most exemplary period in history. Among the women of this time were those who took part in battles in the company of the Prophet himself (peace and blessings be upon him), and after that under the caliphs (rulers) and their commanders.

The Messenger of Allāh (peace and blessings be upon him) told his wife Sawdah, "Allah has permitted you to go out for your needs. If someone's wife asks his permission to go to Allah's House (Masjid), he should not deny it to her. Allah will never humiliate the one who obeys his Lord and takes his Lord as friend and patron."

Indeed Allāh has heard the statement of her (Khawlah bint Tha'labah) that disputes with you (O Muhammad SAW) concerning her husband (Aus bin As-Samit), and complains to Allāh. And Allāh hears the argument between you both. Verily, Allāh is All-Hearer, All-Seer. (58:1)

قَدْ سَمِعَ ٱللَّهُ قَوْلَ ٱلَّتِي تُجَٰدِلُكَ فِي زَوْجِهَا وَتَشْتَكِىٓ إِلَى ٱللَّهِ وَٱللَّهُ يَسْمَعُ تَحَاوُرَكُمَآ إِنَّ ٱللَّهَ سَمِيعٌ بَصِيرٌ ١

Khawlah's story provides a compelling model for how to place Allah Most High at the center of our attempts to find answers to the most difficult questions, and to find relief in the most challenging of situations. It is based on the tafsir (exegetical) literature surrounding the first four verses of Surah al-Mujadilah ("the Arguing Woman").

Khawlah bint Tha'labah was an Ansari woman, from the Medinan tribe of Khazraj. She was married to Aws b. Samit, the brother of the famous Companion 'Ubadah. Unfortunately, Aws was known for having an ill nature, especially as he had gotten older. He was a poor man, weak-sighted, and quick-tempered, some say even slightly mad.

One day, Khawlah was engaged in prayer. As she bent down to make prostration, her husband noticed her shapely figure. As soon as she ended her prayer with the Salam, he asked her to be intimate with him.

She refused, and he went into a rage, instantly pronouncing on her words of Zihar: "You are to me like the back of my mother!" Zihar was a form of divorce used in pre-Islamic Arabia. Men could use certain verbal expressions in which they compared their wives to their mothers, as a way to say, you are now unlawful for me (sexually) just as my mother is. This would result in immediate divorce, and that too of a particularly harsh kind, since the woman would remain stuck in marital limbo. She would not be able to stay married to the husband who pronounced Zihar, nor could she marry anyone else.

However, Aws b. Samit had not really intended to permanently divorce his wife. At this point there are different accounts of what happened next. In one narration, he again tries to be intimate with her, but she pushes him off firmly, exclaiming, "By the One in Whose Hand is the soul of Khuwayla, I will not come to you after you have said what you have said until God and His Messenger decide our case!"

In another account, Khawlah does not initially comprehend the ramifications of Aws' statement. It is he who immediately feels regret, saying "I think you are now forbidden to me," at which point she becomes distraught. In this version, it is Aws who sends her to the Prophet, peace and blessing be upon him, to find out what can be done.

Khawlah went out and asked some of her female neighbors to let her borrow an over garment to wear in front of the Messenger of Allah, peace be upon him. She then rushed to the house of 'Aisha, where she found him.

Her level of distress was obvious. "Verily, Aws married me when I was young and he desired me. Now that I have aged, and worn out my body (by bearing children for him), he has made me like his mother!" She begged the Prophet, peace be upon him, for a solution, hoping he could find a way to have the ruling changed.

However, the Prophet, peace and blessings be upon him, could only reply, "I have nothing (with which I can help you) in your matter. He is forbidden to you." He was cognizant of her pain, but even more conscious of the fact that he, just like she, was a slave of Allah and was required to await His command. Until and unless he was told to do otherwise by divine command, the Prophet, peace be upon him, generally upheld the custom of the pre-Islamic Arabs. Zihar was one such custom. The Zihar of Aws was the first instance to happen among the Muslims, and since the Prophet, peace be upon him, had received no revelation regarding this practice, he treated it as divorce in the same way that the Arabs had always done.

But Khawlah did not let go of the matter. She presented him with argument after argument, hoping to convince him to find a way out of her predicament. Each time the Prophet, peace be upon him, answered in the negative, unable to help her, she had present her case again. "He did not pronounce the word 'talaq' (divorce)," she said.

"He is the father of my child, and the most beloved person to me." "He's made me like his mother, and left me to no one [i.e. with no one to care for me]. Can't you find a legal permission (rukhsa) by which he and I may be relieved?"

The Prophet, peace be upon him, continued to repeat, "You are forbidden to him," and her reasoned arguments increased. "O Messenger of Allah! The customs of the Days of Ignorance have been abrogated [by the coming of Islam], so what about the Zihar my husband has given me?"

Here the Prophet, peace be upon him, replied, "I have not been given any revelation regarding this," to which she said in desperate exasperation, "You are sent revelation on everything, but this matter has been kept hidden from you?" "It is as I have stated," said the Prophet, peace be upon him.

She had tried every logical argument she could think of, but nothing had worked. Finally realizing her complete helplessness and lack of resources, she turned to her Lord. Raising her hands toward the sky, Khawlah began:

"O Allah, it is to You I complain of the severity of my isolation and my grief at this separation!"

"I complain to Allah Most High of my indigence and my terrible state. I have small children. If I give them in custody to him, they will be lost, but if I give them in custody to myself, they will go hungry!"

"O Allah! I complain to You!"

"O Allah, send down [Your revelation] on the tongue of your Prophet (nabi)!"

Her desperate prayers had scarcely ceased that the revelation came down. 'Aisha, the wife of the Prophet, peace be upon him, recognizing what was happening, instructed Khawlah, "Stand back!" "Stay silent!" as he received the Word of God. After some moments, the Prophet, peace upon him, said, "O Khawlah, rejoice!" She asked in trepidation, "Is it good?" Upon which the Messenger of God, peace be upon him, began reciting the following verses:

Certainly has Allah heard the speech of the one who argues with you, [O Muhammad], concerning her husband and directs her complaint to Allah. And Allah hears your dialogue; indeed, Allah is Hearing and Seeing. (58:1)

قَدْ سَمِعَ ٱللَّهُ قَوْلَ ٱلَّتِي تُجَٰدِلُكَ فِي زَوْجِهَا وَتَشْتَكِىٓ إِلَى ٱللَّهِ وَٱللَّهُ يَسْمَعُ تَحَاوُرَكُمَآ إِنَّ ٱللَّهَ سَمِيعٌ بَصِيرٌ ﴿١﴾

Those who pronounce Zihar among you [to separate] from their wives - they are not [consequently] their mothers. Their mothers are none but those who gave birth to them. And indeed, they are saying an objectionable statement and a falsehood. But indeed, Allah is Pardoning and Forgiving. (58:2)

ٱلَّذِينَ يُظَٰهِرُونَ مِنكُم مِّن نِّسَآئِهِم مَّا هُنَّ أُمَّهَٰتِهِمۡۖ إِنۡ أُمَّهَٰتُهُمۡ إِلَّا ٱلَّٰٓـِٔى وَلَدۡنَهُمۡۚ وَإِنَّهُمۡ لَيَقُولُونَ مُنكَرًا مِّنَ ٱلۡقَوۡلِ وَزُورًاۚ وَإِنَّ ٱللَّهَ لَعَفُوٌّ غَفُورٌ ۝

And those who pronounce Zihar from their wives and then [wish to] go back on what they said - then [there must be] the freeing of a slave before they touch one another. That is what you are admonished thereby; and Allah is Acquainted with what you do. (58:3)

وَٱلَّذِينَ يُظَٰهِرُونَ مِن نِّسَآئِهِمۡ ثُمَّ يَعُودُونَ لِمَا قَالُوا۟ فَتَحۡرِيرُ رَقَبَةٍ مِّن قَبۡلِ أَن يَتَمَآسَّاۚ ذَٰلِكُمۡ تُوعَظُونَ بِهِۦۚ وَٱللَّهُ بِمَا تَعۡمَلُونَ خَبِيرٌ ۝

And he who does not find [a slave] - then a fast for two months consecutively before they touch one another; and he who is unable - then the feeding of sixty poor persons. That is for you to believe [completely] in Allah and His Messenger; and those are the limits [set by] Allah. And for the disbelievers is a painful punishment. (Surah al-Mujadalah, 58:4)

فَمَن لَّمْ يَجِدْ فَصِيَامُ شَهْرَيْنِ مُتَتَابِعَيْنِ مِن قَبْلِ أَن يَتَمَآسَّاۖ فَمَن لَّمْ يَسْتَطِعْ فَإِطْعَامُ سِتِّينَ مِسْكِينًاۚ ذَٰلِكَ لِتُؤْمِنُوا بِٱللَّهِ وَرَسُولِهِۦۚ وَتِلْكَ حُدُودُ ٱللَّهِۗ وَلِلْكَٰفِرِينَ عَذَابٌ أَلِيمٌ ۝

By His great mercy of Allah, Khawlah's arguing (mujadalah) then became the impetus for the abrogation of an age-old custom. After receiving the revelation, the Prophet, peace be upon him, called for Aws, and told him to free a slave, but Aws had no slave to set free. The Prophet, peace be upon him, said, then fast two months consecutively, to which Aws replied, "If I don't eat two to three times a day, my weak eyesight turns to blindness."

The Prophet, peace be upon him, said, then feed sixty poor people, to which Aws replied, "I am unable to do so unless you help me with the task." So the Prophet, peace be upon him, and a few other Companions all chipped in until Aws had enough money gathered by which he could feed sixty people, expiate his statement of Zihar, and be reunited with his wife Khawlah.

Through the direct confirmation that Allah Most High had sent her, Sayyidah Khawlah came to have unshaken conviction that taqwa, or having "awe and dread for Allah's might and power, and fear of overstepping His limits," is the key to receiving the mercy of Allah. For this reason, years later, when the Prophet, peace be upon him, had passed away and Omar was caliph and leader over large expanses of the known earth, she was able to convey some of this conviction. She stopped Omar one day in the street and began admonishing him to mind the limits of Allah while ruling over his subjects as caliph:

"Omar! You used to be called Omayr, then you were called Omar, then you were called 'Commander of the Faithful'. Have taqwa of Allah, O Omar! For verily the one who is most certain of death fears loss, and the one most convinced of the Judgment fears punishment."

Omar stood listening to her, and after she parted ways with him, his companions asked why he had allowed "that old woman" to hold him up in such a manner.

He replied, "I swear by Allah, had she held me up from the start of the day till its end, I would not part from her except to do the prescribed prayers. Do you not know who this woman is? She is Khawlah b. Tha'labah. God heard her speech from beyond the seven heavens. [How could it be] that God listens to her speech, and not Omar?"

There are myriad lessons that a scholar or a jurist can draw from this account. What we will focus on here however is something relevant to the contemporary Muslim experience: the fact that in this narrative, we see an early example of a Muslim woman asking for legal change in order to preserve her basic rights and needs. She is a woman who argued for change, and Allah Most High listened and granted her what she desired.

One might be urged to say: "Sayyida Khawlah was the first Muslim feminist!" She might have unjustly refused the sexual right of her husband, but the punishment she received certainly did not fit the crime. For this reason, she was convinced in her heart that she deserved better from Allah, and from His Messenger, peace be upon him, and from the Shari'ah with which he was sent.

But this is not a feminist story. The experience of Sayyida Khawlah is far, far removed from feminism, both in terms of time and in terms of spiritual reality. Feminism originated during a moment of history when the focus of human societies began to turn away from the rights of God toward the rights of the individual. The main focus of feminism is empowerment, autonomy, freedom, and it calls on women to not only know their rights but to demand them with vehemence out of a sense of sheer entitlement. According to this philosophy, the more the individual is empowered, the better, even if that risks the disruption of critical social institutions such as family, community, religious authority, and social harmony. And in this process, the right of God to decide what is good and true and best for one is slowly, over time, completely sidelined, in favor of what each human individual decides for himself as to what is better. Therefore, the story of Sayyida Khawlah is anything but this. It is a story in which every actor demonstrates not their autonomy but their submission: the wife through her seeking a religious solution from the Prophet, peace and blessings be upon him, by anxiously awaiting the judgment of Allah in the matter, and the husband by complying with the fact that he must pay expiation to appease God for his actions. The members of the community comply as well: the other Companions of the Prophet, peace be upon him, acknowledged the weakness of their brother, and helped him make up for his rash action, rather than show him disdain.

Even Khawlah's argumentation is a type of submission, because the scholars of Qur'anic exegesis make clear that mujadala or argumentation can be of two types: that which is on the side of Falsehood, and undertaken only so that one can overcome one's opponent; or that which is done with the intention of bringing the Truth to light. By the submission shown by all involved, one can imagine concentric circles of relationships of family, community, and religious authority, tying one to another to make a wholesome edifice that submits itself as entirely as possible to Allah, even in times of trial. Instead of empowerment, this incident teaches us humble submission.

Instead of an aggressive individualism, it teaches us to seek our rights but to do so by maintaining the connections that are obligatory for us to maintain. Filtered through the lens of seeking empowerment, all we can see in this story is injustice and delayed gratification. But read through the lens of humble submission, we see a surprising amount of mercy: Sayyida Khawlah's love and commitment to a husband she understands to be at times exasperatingly temperamental; Sayyiduna Aws' coming forward to make amends before the Prophet, peace be upon him, and his other companions, despite his manly pride; and the Prophet, peace be upon him, joyous when the pleas of the desperate woman are heard by Allah Most High. Imam al-Qushayri, in his Sufi commentary of the Qur'an says about Sayyida Khawlah, the "Arguing Woman": "The moment her complaint became truly directed to Allah alone, and she despaired of anyone else removing her difficulty save Him, is the moment when Allah sent down [the verses beginning with the words] 'Allah Has Heard' to clarify her matter." Sayyida Khawlah teaches us that it is not wrong to "argue."

We learn from her example that there is no shame in asking questions and seeking justice. But the biggest lesson we learn from her is that when seeking justice or when engaged in any argument, we must always put Allah first. At the very moment when she finally put Him first in her heart did her deliverance from the trial come. And from then on, having taqwa took on an urgency that she could not bear but to communicate with others, because she understood at a very deep level the following: And for those who fear Allah, He (ever) prepares a way out, And He provides for him from (sources) he never could imagine. And if anyone puts his trust in Allah, sufficient is ((Allah)) for him. (65:2-3) Her submission before her Lord, and His answering of her pleas, was so powerful that even Omar, the most prominent political leader of the time, could not turn away from her admonishment and advice. Her consciousness of Allah and His Right had become so strong that she could not resist reminding anyone she saw of the need to submit to Him. And her sincerity and light were so great that one could not easily resist her calls to the Truth.

It is due to the truth of His Absolute Justice that man must be careful in his relationships. Yes, power discrepancies lend themselves to abuse, but they also allow for the actualization of the highest of human potential. Allah subhanahu wa ta'ala says in the chapter on Women (al-Nisa'):

Indeed, Allah commands you to render trusts to whom they are due and when you judge between people to judge with justice. Excellent is that which Allah instructs you. Indeed, Allah is ever Hearing and Seeing. (4:58)

$$\text{﴿ إِنَّ اللَّهَ يَأْمُرُكُمْ أَن تُؤَدُّوا الْأَمَانَاتِ إِلَىٰ أَهْلِهَا وَإِذَا حَكَمْتُم بَيْنَ النَّاسِ أَن تَحْكُمُوا بِالْعَدْلِ إِنَّ اللَّهَ نِعِمَّا يَعِظُكُم بِهِ إِنَّ اللَّهَ كَانَ سَمِيعًا بَصِيرًا ﴾ (٥٨)}$$

Allah, the Almighty, created His slaves to test which is best in deed. He provided sustenance for them so that they may be grateful to Him. Nevertheless, many men and women have worshipped other than Him and the masses are thankful not to Him, but to others, because the characteristic of ingratitude is widespread among human beings.

Therefore, do not be depressed when you find that your family, friends, son or daughter forget your kindness. Some people might even loathe you and make you an enemy for no reason at all. From among the ever-repeating stories of history is a story of a mother and her daughter: the former raised her, fed her, clothed her and taught her she would stay up nights so that her daughter could sleep, stay hungry so that her daughter could eat, and she would toil as a maid so that her daughter could feel comfort.

However, when the daughter became stronger and older, she rewarded her mother and father with disobedience, disrespect, and contempt. Always remember that Allah will never forget you. So be at peace if you are requited with ungratefulness for the great deeds that you have done.

Rejoice in your knowledge that you will be rewarded from Allah always, the One Who has everything, unlimited treasures at His disposal. But you should not stop from doing acts of kindness towards others: the point is that you should always be prepared for ingratitude.

Perform acts of kindness and charity seeking Allah's pleasure, because with this attitude you will assuredly be successful in this life and the next. The ungrateful person can never harm you: praise Allah that this person is the sinner and that you are the obedient servant. Always remember that the hand that gives is better than the hand that receives. "We feed you only for the countenance of Allah. We wish not from you reward or gratitude. (76:9)

إِنَّمَا نُطْعِمُكُمْ لِوَجْهِ اللَّهِ لَا نُرِيدُ مِنكُمْ جَزَآءً وَلَا شُكُورًا ﴿٩﴾

Many people are often shocked at the nature of ingratitude in others, as though they had never come across this verse and others like it: And when affliction touches man, he calls upon Us, whether lying on his side or sitting or standing; but when We remove from him his affliction, he continues [in disobedience] as if he had never called upon Us to [remove] an affliction that touched him. Thus is made pleasing to the transgressors that which they have been doing. (10:12)

وَإِذَا مَسَّ ٱلْإِنسَـٰنَ ٱلضُّرُّ دَعَانَا لِجَنبِهِۦ أَوْ قَاعِدًا أَوْ قَآئِمًا فَلَمَّا كَشَفْنَا عَنْهُ ضُرَّهُۥ مَرَّ كَأَن لَّمْ يَدْعُنَآ إِلَىٰ ضُرٍّ مَّسَّهُۥ كَذَٰلِكَ زُيِّنَ لِلْمُسْرِفِينَ مَا كَانُوا۟ يَعْمَلُونَ ١٢

Hence do not be in a state of anger if you give a friend a book as a gift but she strikes you with it. Most human beings are ungrateful to their Creator, so what treatment should you expect?

The Ways of Attaining Faith in Allāh

"Happiness is attained by three things: being patient when tested, being thankful when receiving a blessing, and being repentant upon sinning."

Those who have faith and work righteousness, they are companions of the Garden: Therein shall they abide (Forever). (2:82)

وَٱلَّذِينَ ءَامَنُوا۟ وَعَمِلُوا۟ ٱلصَّٰلِحَٰتِ أُو۟لَٰٓئِكَ أَصْحَٰبُ ٱلْجَنَّةِ هُمْ فِيهَا خَٰلِدُونَ ﴿٨٢﴾

When any person looks at anything, he notices every particle in this life requires a cause for its existence, it either gives existence to itself or something gives it existence. But if it is not possible for it to give existence to itself, how could it give existence to anything else? Look at a tree, from its stem to the leaves; indeed, it is a marvelous beauty that amazes the intellects.

What gave each one of the cells of the leaves the power to absorb water and nourishment from the depths of the earth? "He causes it to grow for you. Indeed in it is a sign for a people who give thought." (16:11)

$$يُنۢبِتُ لَكُم بِهِ ٱلزَّرْعَ وَٱلزَّيْتُونَ وَٱلنَّخِيلَ وَٱلْأَعْنَٰبَ وَمِن كُلِّ ٱلثَّمَرَٰتِ ۗ إِنَّ فِى ذَٰلِكَ لَءَايَةً لِّقَوْمٍ يَتَفَكَّرُونَ ﴿١١﴾$$

"And who believe in what has been revealed to you, [O Muhammad], and what was revealed before you, and of the Hereafter they are certain [in faith]." (2:4)

$$وَٱلَّذِينَ يُؤْمِنُونَ بِمَآ أُنزِلَ إِلَيْكَ وَمَآ أُنزِلَ مِن قَبْلِكَ وَبِٱلْءَاخِرَةِ هُمْ يُوقِنُونَ ﴿٤﴾$$

We have no choice in this life but to do good deeds, like acts of worship and prayer. One must always put all their trust in God and submitting to His will always.

If Allāh helps you, none can overcome you; and if He forsakes you, who is there after Him that can help you? And in Allāh (Alone) let believers put their trust. (3:160)

إِن يَنصُرْكُمُ ٱللَّهُ فَلَا غَالِبَ لَكُمْ وَإِن يَخْذُلْكُمْ فَمَن ذَا ٱلَّذِى يَنصُرُكُم مِّنۢ بَعْدِهِۦ ۗ وَعَلَى ٱللَّهِ فَلْيَتَوَكَّلِ ٱلْمُؤْمِنُونَ ﴿١٦٠﴾

The story of Hajar gives all of us the most beautiful example of the deep faith in God (Allāh) and sincere trust in Him. Prophet Ibrahim, May peace be upon him always, left his wife at the House of Allāh in Makkah, above the well of Zamzam. At that time there were no people and no water there at all. Hajar had no-one with her except her baby son, Ismail. She asked her husband Ibrahim, calmly and kindly: "Has God commanded you to leave us here?" Ibrahim replied, "Yes!" Her response showed her acceptance and optimism: "Then God is not going to abandon us."

Our Lord, I have settled some of my descendants in an uncultivated valley near Your sacred House, our Lord, that they may establish prayer. So make hearts among the people incline toward them and provide for them from the fruits that they might be grateful. (14:37)

رَبَّنَآ إِنِّىٓ أَسْكَنتُ مِن ذُرِّيَّتِى بِوَادٍ غَيْرِ ذِى زَرْعٍ عِندَ بَيْتِكَ ٱلْمُحَرَّمِ رَبَّنَا لِيُقِيمُوا۟ ٱلصَّلَوٰةَ فَٱجْعَلْ أَفْـِٔدَةً مِّنَ ٱلنَّاسِ تَهْوِىٓ إِلَيْهِمْ وَٱرْزُقْهُم مِّنَ ٱلثَّمَرَٰتِ لَعَلَّهُمْ يَشْكُرُونَ ﴿٣٧﴾

Here was a truly difficult situation: a man leaving his wife and baby son in a barren, hot, and dry land, where there were no plants, not even water, animals, or anyone. Ibrahim was told to go back to the distant land of Palestine without his wife and son. He left nothing with Hajar but a small sack of dates (fruit) and a skin filled with very little water. Were it not for her deep faith and trust in Allah that filled her heart, Hajar would not have been able to cope with such a sad situation.

She would have fainted straight away, and would not have become the strong woman whose name is forever remembered. For example, each time a Muslim performs hajj or umrah at the House of God, they drink the pure water of Zamzam, and run between the mounts of Safa and Marwah remembering Hajar, as Hajar done on that most difficult day. Through the many centuries, Hajar's deep faith and her love of God had an amazing effect on the lives of men and women. Hajar awoke their consciences and reminded them that God knows every secret, and that He is with you wherever you may be. It is impossible to hide from God.

Narrated Abdullah ibn Zayd ibn Aslam, his grandfather said: `One day when I was accompanying Omar on his patrol at night, Omar felt tired, so he put his back against some wall. It was a dark without a moon, then we heard a woman saying to her daughter, "My daughter, stand-up and mix the milk with some water."

Then her daughter said, "Mother, you did not hear the decree of Omar (chief of the believers) today?" The mother said, "What Omar said?" The daughter said, "He ordered his assistant to announce that milk must never be mixed with water." The mother said, "Just mix the milk with water; you are in my house, Omar cannot see you." Her daughter replied, "But God sees everything." `Omar heard this, and said "Go to that house and see who is that girl and whether she has a husband?"

So I went to that house, and I learned that she was not married. The other woman was her mother. I came to Omar and told him the story.

He called his sons, and said to them: "Do any of you need a good wife? If I was younger and I had the desire to get married, I would marry this beautiful hearted woman." Abdullah said: "I have a good wife." Abd al-Rahman said: "I also have a good wife." Asim said: "Father, I do not have a wife, so please let me marry her."

So Omar arranged for her to be married to his son Asim. She gave him a daughter, who grew up to be the mother of Omar ibn Abd al-Aziz.''' Omar al-Aziz became a caliph and ruled from 717 to 720. This young woman was righteous and honest in all her deeds, both in public and in private, because she believed that God was with her at all times and God sees and hears everything. This is true faith (Emman). One of the immediate rewards that God gave her was this blessed marriage.

A true and pure faith increases the character and weight of a woman in maturity, strength, and understanding, so she sees earthly life clearly. Life is just a place of worship and testing. The results will be seen on the Day of Judgment. On that Day, all of mankind will be brought in front of God to account for their deeds. If their deeds are good, it will be good for them. Allah is fair in His judgment. There will not be the slightest injustice: On that Day, every soul will be rewarded for what it earned. No injustice will there be on that Day. (40:17)

ٱلۡيَوۡمَ تُجۡزَىٰ كُلُّ نَفۡسِۭ بِمَا كَسَبَتۡ لَا ظُلۡمَ ٱلۡيَوۡمَ إِنَّ ٱللَّهَ سَرِيعُ ٱلۡحِسَابِ ﴿١٧﴾

On that Day, every deed will be measured to the utmost precision. If anyone did an atom's weight of good, then they shall see it! And if anyone did an atom's weight of evil, they shall see it. (99:7-8)

فَمَن يَعۡمَلۡ مِثۡقَالَ ذَرَّةٍ خَيۡرٗا يَرَهُۥ ﴿٧﴾ وَمَن يَعۡمَلۡ مِثۡقَالَ ذَرَّةٖ شَرّٗا يَرَهُۥ ﴿٨﴾

And We place the scales of justice for the Day of Resurrection, so no soul will be treated unjustly at all. And if there is [even] the weight of a mustard seed, We will bring it forth. And sufficient are We as accountant. (21:47)

وَنَضَعُ ٱلۡمَوَٰزِينَ ٱلۡقِسۡطَ لِيَوۡمِ ٱلۡقِيَٰمَةِ فَلَا تُظۡلَمُ نَفۡسٞ شَيۡـٔٗاۖ وَإِن كَانَ مِثۡقَالَ حَبَّةٖ مِّنۡ خَرۡدَلٍ أَتَيۡنَا بِهَاۗ وَكَفَىٰ بِنَا حَٰسِبِينَ ﴿٤٧﴾

No misfortune can happen on earth or to you but is recorded in a decree before We bring it into existence: That is easy for Allah. (57: 22)

مَآ أَصَابَ مِن مُّصِيبَةٍ فِي ٱلْأَرْضِ وَلَا فِيٓ أَنفُسِكُمْ إِلَّا فِى كِتَٰبٍ مِّن قَبْلِ أَن نَّبْرَأَهَآ إِنَّ ذَٰلِكَ عَلَى ٱللَّهِ يَسِيرٌ ﴿٢٢﴾

So remember that the pen has dried, the pages have already been written: all events that shall come to pass have already been set in stone. Never will we be struck except by what Allah has decreed for us; He is our protector. And upon Allah let the believers rely. (9:51)

قُل لَّن يُصِيبَنَآ إِلَّا مَا كَتَبَ ٱللَّهُ لَنَا هُوَ مَوْلَىٰنَا وَعَلَى ٱللَّهِ فَلْيَتَوَكَّلِ ٱلْمُؤْمِنُونَ ﴿٥١﴾

So whatever has befallen you was not meant to escape you, and whatever has escaped you was not meant for you. If this belief is strongly ingrained in your heart, then all hardship and struggles would become ease and comfort.

The Prophet, peace and blessings be upon him, said: "Whoever Allah loves and wishes good for, He inflicts him (with hardship)."

For this reason, do not feel overly troubled if you are afflicted with sickness, the death of a daughter, mother, or a loss in wealth. Allah has decreed these matters to occur for a reason and the decisions are His, and His alone. When we truly have this faith, we shall be rewarded well and our sins shall be atoned for. So for those that are afflicted with disaster, good news await them: so remain patient and happy. He is not questioned about what He does, but they will be questioned. (21:23)

لَا يُسْئَلُ عَمَّا يَفْعَلُ وَهُمْ يُسْئَلُونَ ۝

You will never completely feel happy until you truly believe that Allah has already preordained everything and all matters. The pen's ink has dried and with it has been written everything that will happen to you in this life and the next.

Therefore do not feel sorrow over that which is not in your hands. Do not think that you could have prevented the horse from falling, the rain from flooding, the wind from blowing, or the cat from dying. You could not have prevented these things, whether you wanted to or not. All that has been written shall come to pass.

And say: "*The truth is from your Lord, so whoever wills - let him believe; and whoever wills - let him disbelieve.*" Indeed, We have prepared for the wrongdoers a fire whose walls will surround them. And if they call for relief, they will be relieved with water like murky oil, which scalds [their] faces. Wretched is the drink, and evil is the resting place. (18:29)

وَقُلِ ٱلْحَقُّ مِن رَّبِّكُمْ فَمَن شَاءَ فَلْيُؤْمِن وَمَن شَاءَ فَلْيَكْفُرْ إِنَّا أَعْتَدْنَا لِلظَّالِمِينَ نَارًا أَحَاطَ بِهِمْ سُرَادِقُهَا وَإِن يَسْتَغِيثُوا يُغَاثُوا بِمَاءٍ كَٱلْمُهْلِ يَشْوِي ٱلْوُجُوهَ بِئْسَ ٱلشَّرَابُ وَسَاءَتْ مُرْتَفَقًا ﴿٢٩﴾

So surrender yourself: believe in what has been
written, before pains of anger and regret engulf
you. If you have done all that was in your
power, and afteiwards what you had been
striving against still takes place, have firm faith
that it was meant to be. So never think or say:
"had I done this, such-and-such would have
never happened to me." Rather say: "this is the
decree of Allah, and what He wishes, He does."

قُل لَّن يُصِيبَنَا إِلَّا مَا كَتَبَ ٱللَّهُ لَنَا هُوَ مَوْلَىٰنَا ۚ وَعَلَى ٱللَّهِ فَلْيَتَوَكَّلِ ٱلْمُؤْمِنُونَ ﴿٥١﴾

Verily, with every difficulty there is relief. So
when you have finished [your duties], then
stand up [for worship]. And to your Lord
direct [your] longing. (94:6-8)

إِنَّ مَعَ ٱلْعُسْرِ يُسْرًا ﴿٦﴾
فَإِذَا فَرَغْتَ فَٱنصَبْ ﴿٧﴾
وَإِلَىٰ رَبِّكَ فَٱرْغَب ﴿٨﴾

Breathing follows exhalation, drinking follows thirst, sleep comes after a long day, and health takes the place of illness. The lost will find their way, the one in difficulty will find support and relief, the day will follow the night, and death will follow life. No one can stop what Allah has decreed.

So you see those in whose hearts is disease hastening into [association with] them, saying, "We are afraid a misfortune may strike us." But perhaps Allah will bring conquest or a decision from Him, and they will become, over what they have been concealing within themselves, regretful. (5:52)

فَتَرَى ٱلَّذِينَ فِى قُلُوبِهِم مَّرَضٌ يُسَٰرِعُونَ فِيهِمْ يَقُولُونَ نَخْشَىٰٓ أَن تُصِيبَنَا دَآئِرَةٌ فَعَسَى ٱللَّهُ أَن يَأْتِىَ بِٱلْفَتْحِ أَوْ أَمْرٍ مِّنْ عِندِهِۦ فَيُصْبِحُوا۟ عَلَىٰ مَآ أَسَرُّوا۟ فِىٓ أَنفُسِهِمْ نَٰدِمِينَ ﴿٥٢﴾

If you see that the desert extend for a hundred miles, then know that beyond that distance are blue rivers, green meadows, trees and shade. If you see the rope tighten and tighten around you, know that it will eventually snap.

Tear drops are followed by laughter and relief, fear is replaced by comfort and courage, and anxiety is overthrown by peace and serenity. When the fire was prepared for him, Prophet Abraham, peace be upon him, did not fear its flames. Allah said: "O fire, be coolness and safety upon Abraham." (21:69)

قُلْنَا يَـٰنَارُ كُونِى بَرْدًا وَسَلَـٰمًا عَلَىٰٓ إِبْرَٰهِيـمَ ﴿٦٩﴾

The Red Sea and its waters could not drown Prophet Moses, peace be upon him, because his faith was strong. He spoke in a strong and firm voice: "No! Indeed, with me is my Lord; He will guide me." (26:62)

قَالَ كَلَّآ إِنَّ مَعِىَ رَبِّى سَيَهْدِينِ ﴿٦٢﴾

Prophet Muhammad, peace be upon him, told Abu Bakr in the cave that Allah was with them, then peace and tranquility descended upon them. Moses also said, "No! Indeed, with me is my Lord; He will guide me." (26:62)

قَالَ كَلَّآ إِنَّ مَعِىَ رَبِّى سَيَهْدِينِ ﴿٦٢﴾

Those that are slaves and sad of the moment will see only misery and pain. This is because the person looks only at the wall, windows, and door of the room, whereas they should look beyond such barriers. If Allah touch thee with affliction, none can remove it but He; if He touch thee with happiness, He hath power over all things. (6:17)

وَإِن يَمْسَسْكَ ٱللَّهُ بِضُرٍّ فَلَا كَاشِفَ لَهُۥ إِلَّا هُوَ وَإِن يَمْسَسْكَ بِخَيْرٍ فَهُوَ عَلَىٰ كُلِّ شَىْءٍ قَدِيرٌ ﴿١٧﴾

Therefore do not be in despair. It is impossible for anything to remain the same. Time never stops. The days, weeks, and years rotate, the future is still unseen, and every day Allah has matters to bring forth.

Allah will afterwards bring some new thing to pass. Allah told us that with any hardship, there is relief (i.e. there is one hardship with two reliefs, so one hardship cannot overcome two reliefs). (94:5)

فَإِنَّ مَعَ الْعُسْرِ يُسْرًا ۝

She Worships God (Allāh) Alone

There are 6 stages to knowledge:

1. Ask questions in a good manner,
2. Remain quiet and listen attentively,
3. Understand well,
4. Memorize,
5. Teach, and
6. Act upon the knowledge and keep to its limits.

A good woman worships her Lord each day. She worship no other besides Him. She knows that she must observe and obey all of His commandments. She offers each of the prayers on time. She does not invent excuses, and never let her chores prevent her from praying on time. Worship and prayer are the pillar of religion, and whoever neglects prayer destroys the faith. Prayer is the most noble of deeds.

As long as you are performing prayer, you are knocking at the door of Allah, and whoever is knocking at the door of Allah, Allah will open it for him. A slave stands in front of Allah on two occasions:

- The first during Salah,
- And secondly on the Day of Judgment.

Whosoever stands correctly in the first, the second standing will be made easier for him. And whosoever, disregards the first standing, the second standing will be very difficult.

The Prophet, Peace and Blessing be upon him, was asked: 'What deed is most loved by God (Allāh)?' The Prophet replied: "to offer each prayer on time, and to treat your own parents with lots of respect and mercy." Prayer is the rope that pulls God and man together. It is the link between the servant and the Lord. It is like a well from which a person pulls their thirst and nourishment, and gets strength, contentment, and cleanses the stains of sin.

The Messenger of Allāh (peace and blessings be upon him) said: "What would you say if there was a beautiful river running by your door, and you bathed in it at least 5 times a day, would any dirt be left on you?" The people said: "No!" The Prophet said: "This is exactly like the 5 daily prayers, through which Allāh erases sins. If you knew the true value of yourself, you will never allow yourself to be humiliated by committing sins."

And seek help through patience and prayer, and indeed, it is difficult except for the humbly submissive [to Allāh] (2:45)

وَٱسْتَعِينُوا۟ بِٱلصَّبْرِ وَٱلصَّلَوٰةِ ۚ وَإِنَّهَا لَكَبِيرَةٌ إِلَّا عَلَى ٱلْخَٰشِعِينَ ﴿٤٥﴾

If a woman's patience is stronger than her whims and desires, then she is like an angel, but if her whims and desires are stronger than her patience, then her abode is the hellfire. If her desire for food, drink and sex is stronger than her patience, then she no better than the devil.

Prayer makes us better. Prayer is a mercy, which Allah has bestowed upon His creation. We seek its shade 5 times a day and praise God, glorifying Him, and asking for His help, mercy, guidance, and forgiveness. So prayer is a means of purification for those who pray. Prayer washes our sins away. So establish prayer and give zakat, and whatever good you put forward for yourselves, you will find it with Allāh. Indeed, Allāh of what you do, is Seeing. (2:110)

وَأَقِيمُوا۟ ٱلصَّلَوٰةَ وَءَاتُوا۟ ٱلزَّكَوٰةَ وَمَا نُقَدِّمُوا۟ لِأَنفُسِكُم مِّنْ خَيْرٍ تَجِدُوهُ عِندَ ٱللَّهِ إِنَّ ٱللَّهَ بِمَا تَعْمَلُونَ بَصِيرٌ ﴿١١٠﴾

The Prophet (peace and blessings be upon him) said: "When the time for prayer comes, if you do good wudu (wash) properly, then you concentrate on the prayer and bow correctly, your prayer will then be an expiation for the sins committed prior to it, as long as you committed no major sins. This is the case until the end." (Sahih Muslim 3/112).

You have a perfect example in the Prophet, peace and blessings be upon him. The entrails of a camel were placed upon his head, but the Prophet continued to pray in front of his enemies. The Prophet was a perfect model to his followers. His feet bled often. He was hit and his face was fractured. He was surrounded in a mountain pass until he was forced to eat tree leaves. He was driven out of Makkah; his teeth were broken in a battle; his innocent wife was accused of wrongdoing; seventy of his Companions were killed; he was bereaved of his son and of most of his daughters; he would even tie a stone around his stomach to lessen the pangs of hunger; and he was accused of being a poet, a soothsayer, a madman, and a liar all at the same time. Yet Allah protected him throughout these severe trials and tribulations. Prophet Zakariyah (Zacharia) was killed. His son, Prophet Yahiya (John), was slaughtered, Prophet Moses was afflicted with great trials, and Prophet Abraham was thrown into the fire, (peace and blessings be upon them all). Many scholars of today and of the past have been flogged, imprisoned, or tortured.

Or do you think that you will enter Paradise while such [trial] has not yet come to you as came to those who passed on before you? They were touched by poverty and hardship and were shaken until [even their] messenger and those who believed with him said, "When is the help of Allah?" Unquestionably, the help of (2:214)

أَمْ حَسِبْتُمْ أَن تَدْخُلُوا۟ ٱلْجَنَّةَ وَلَمَّا يَأْتِكُم مَّثَلُ ٱلَّذِينَ خَلَوْا۟ مِن قَبْلِكُم مَّسَّتْهُمُ ٱلْبَأْسَاءُ وَٱلضَّرَّاءُ وَزُلْزِلُوا۟ حَتَّىٰ يَقُولَ ٱلرَّسُولُ وَٱلَّذِينَ ءَامَنُوا۟ مَعَهُۥ مَتَىٰ نَصْرُ ٱللَّهِ أَلَآ إِنَّ نَصْرَ ٱللَّهِ قَرِيبٌ ۝

[He] who created death and life to test you [as to] which of you is best in deed - and He is the Exalted in Might, the Forgiving. (67:2)

ٱلَّذِى خَلَقَ ٱلْمَوْتَ وَٱلْحَيَوٰةَ لِيَبْلُوَكُمْ أَيُّكُمْ أَحْسَنُ عَمَلًا وَهُوَ ٱلْعَزِيزُ ٱلْغَفُورُ ۝

By earnestly doing the 5 daily prayers, you will achieve the greatest of blessings: atonement for your sins and an increase in rank with our Lord. Prayer is a very potent remedy for sicknesses. Prayer instills faith in your soul. As for those that keep away from the Masjid and away from the prayer, for them are great unhappiness, wretchedness, and an embittered life. But those who disbelieve - for them is misery, and He will waste their deeds. (47:8)

وَٱلَّذِينَ كَفَرُوا۟ فَتَعْسًا لَّهُمْ وَأَضَلَّ أَعْمَالَهُمْ ﴿٨﴾

Those to whom hypocrites said, "Indeed, the people have gathered against you, so fear them." But it [merely] increased them in faith, and they said, "Sufficient for us is Allah, and [He is] the best Disposer of affairs." (3: 173)

ٱلَّذِينَ قَالَ لَهُمُ ٱلنَّاسُ إِنَّ ٱلنَّاسَ قَدْ جَمَعُوا۟ لَكُمْ فَٱخْشَوْهُمْ فَزَادَهُمْ إِيمَٰنًا وَقَالُوا۟ حَسْبُنَا ٱللَّهُ وَنِعْمَ ٱلْوَكِيلُ ﴿١٧٣﴾

By leaving your affairs to Allah, by depending upon Him, by trusting in His promise, by being pleased with His decree, by thinking favorably of Allah, and by waiting patiently for His help, you harvest some of the greater fruits of faith and display the more prominent characteristics of the true believer. When you incorporate these good qualities into your character, you will be at peace concerning the future, because you will depend on Allah for everything. As a result, you will find care, help, protection, and victory always.

Women may attend the Jamaah (Congregational) Prayer in the Masjid

Allāh has exempted all women from the obligation to attend Friday prayer in the masjid. However, women may attend prayer if they want to, but must dress well so not to cause temptations. And indeed, the first women in Islam did pray in the masjid behind the Prophet (peace and blessings be upon him).

Aisha (May Allāh be pleased with her) (the wife of the Prophet) said: "The Messenger of Allāh (peace and blessings be upon him) used to pray Fajr (Morning Prayer), and the believing women prayed behind him. They were wrapped up in their outer garments, and afterwards they went back to their homes, and no Muslim man bothered them."

O Prophet, tell your wives and your daughters and the women of the believers to bring down over themselves [part] of their outer garments.

That is more suitable that they will be known and not be abused. And ever is Allah Forgiving and Merciful. (33:59)

يَـٰٓأَيُّهَا ٱلنَّبِىُّ قُل لِّأَزْوَٰجِكَ وَبَنَاتِكَ وَنِسَآءِ ٱلْمُؤْمِنِينَ يُدْنِينَ عَلَيْهِنَّ مِن جَلَـٰبِيبِهِنَّ ذَٰلِكَ أَدْنَىٰٓ أَن يُعْرَفْنَ فَلَا يُؤْذَيْنَ وَكَانَ ٱللَّهُ غَفُورًا رَّحِيمًا ﴿٥٩﴾

The Prophet (peace be upon him) always shortened the prayer if he heard a baby or child crying. The Prophet (peace and blessings be upon him) said: "I always began each prayer intending to make it lengthy, but if I heard a child crying, I shortened the prayer, because I knew the stress the mother might be feeling because of the crying. Allāh showed great mercy to all women by sparing them from offering the five compulsory prayers in congregation, in the masjid. If Allāh had made it obligatory on women as well, then it would have placed a tough burden on many women, and they may not have been able to do it, as we can see many men failing to pray on a regular basis in the masjid."

If woman asks her husband for permission to go to the masjid, her husband is not allowed to stop her, as the Prophet said in a number of hadith: "Even though their houses are better for them, do not stop your women from going to the masjid. If the wife of any man wants to go to the masjid, do not stop her."

The men of that time, heeded the words and command of the Prophet (peace and blessings be upon him), and allowed their women to go out to the masjid, even if it was against their own wishes. There is no clearer sign of this matter than the hadith of Abdullah ibn Omar, in which he said: Omar's wife used to pray Fajr and Isha prayers in the masjid, and she was asked: "Why do you go to the masjid when you know that your husband, Omar, dislikes this and he is also a very jealous man?" She said: "What is stopping Omar from stopping me?" They said: "the words of the Messenger of Allāh (peace and blessings be upon him): never stop any female servants of Allāh from attending the masjid of Allāh."

The Prophet allowed women to attend the masjid, and prohibited men from stopping them from doing so. The Masjid became full of women coming and going, both at the time of the Prophet (peace be upon him), and in later periods.

Indeed, the Muslim men and Muslim women, the believing men and believing women, the obedient men and obedient women, the truthful men and truthful women, the patient men and patient women, the humble men and humble women, the charitable men and charitable women, the fasting men and fasting women, the men who guard their private parts and the women who do so, and the men who remember Allah often and the women who do so - for them Allah has prepared forgiveness and a great reward. (33:35)

إِنَّ ٱلْمُسْلِمِينَ وَٱلْمُسْلِمَٰتِ وَٱلْمُؤْمِنِينَ وَٱلْمُؤْمِنَٰتِ
وَٱلْقَٰنِتِينَ وَٱلْقَٰنِتَٰتِ وَٱلصَّٰدِقِينَ وَٱلصَّٰدِقَٰتِ وَٱلصَّٰبِرِينَ
وَٱلصَّٰبِرَٰتِ وَٱلْخَٰشِعِينَ وَٱلْخَٰشِعَٰتِ وَٱلْمُتَصَدِّقِينَ
وَٱلْمُتَصَدِّقَٰتِ وَٱلصَّٰٓئِمِينَ وَٱلصَّٰٓئِمَٰتِ وَٱلْحَٰفِظِينَ
فُرُوجَهُمْ وَٱلْحَٰفِظَٰتِ وَٱلذَّٰكِرِينَ ٱللَّهَ كَثِيرًا
وَٱلذَّٰكِرَٰتِ أَعَدَّ ٱللَّهُ لَهُم مَّغْفِرَةً وَأَجْرًا عَظِيمًا ﴿٣٥﴾

Many women went to pray, listen to lectures, and took part in the public life of Islam. When the command from Allāh came to take the Kabbah as the new qiblah (the direction to turn during prayer), the men and women who were praying and facing towards Palestine, turned to face the direction of the Kabbah.

This means that the women and men that were praying together, had to change places. The masjid is the center of light and guidance for men and women. From the dawn of Islam, women had their role to play in the masjid.

There are many sahih reports and books that confirm the woman's presence and their role in the masjid. The reports describe how women attended regular prayer, the Eid prayers, the eclipse prayer, and responding to the call of the muezzin to join the prayer.

The Prophet (peace and blessings be upon) taught everyone to present a clean appearance at Friday and all prayers by encouraging them to take a shower. The Prophet said: "Whoever comes to the prayer, men or women, they should take a shower first."

Hadith reports also tell us about Asma bint, daughter of Abu Bakr (May Allāh be pleased with her). She attended the eclipse prayer (salat al-kusuf) with the Prophet (peace and blessings be upon him). Asma could not hear the Prophet's words clearly, so she asked a man who was nearby what the Prophet said.

This hadith is reported by Bukhari: The Messenger of Allāh (peace be upon him) stood up to address the people (after the eclipse prayer), and spoke about the testing that all humans will undergo in the grave. When he mentioned that, the people panicked and were loud, and so this prevented Asma from hearing the latter part of the Prophet's speech. When the noise died down, Asma asked a man who was nearby, `May Allāh bless you, what did the Messenger of Allāh say?' The main said, "It was revealed to the Prophet (peace be upon him) that everyone will be tested in the grave with something similar in severity to the test (fitnah) of the Dajjal.''

And verily, for those who do wrong, there is another punishment (i.e. the torment in this world and in their graves) before this, but most of them know not. (52:47)

وَإِنَّ لِلَّذِينَ ظَلَمُوا۟ عَذَابًا دُونَ ذَٰلِكَ وَلَٰكِنَّ أَكْثَرَهُمْ لَا يَعْلَمُونَ ﴿٤٧﴾

Indeed, your Lord knows, [O Muhammad], that you stand [in prayer] almost two thirds of the night or half of it or a third of it, and [so do] a group of those with you. And Allah determines [the extent of] the night and the day. He has known that you [Muslims] will not be able to do it and has turned to you in forgiveness, so recite what is easy [for you] of the Qur'an. He has known that there will be among you those who are ill and others traveling throughout the land seeking [something] of the bounty of Allah and others fighting for the cause of Allah. So recite what is easy from it and establish prayer and give zakat and loan Allah a goodly loan. And whatever good you put forward for yourselves - you will find it with Allah. It is better and greater in reward. And seek forgiveness of Allah. Indeed, Allah is Forgiving and Merciful. (73:20)

۞ إِنَّ رَبَّكَ يَعْلَمُ أَنَّكَ تَقُومُ أَدْنَىٰ مِن ثُلُثَيِ ٱلَّيْلِ وَنِصْفَهُۥ وَثُلُثَهُۥ وَطَآئِفَةٌ مِّنَ
ٱلَّذِينَ مَعَكَ وَٱللَّهُ يُقَدِّرُ ٱلَّيْلَ وَٱلنَّهَارَ عَلِمَ أَن لَّن تُحْصُوهُ فَتَابَ عَلَيْكُمْ
فَٱقْرَءُوا مَا تَيَسَّرَ مِنَ ٱلْقُرْءَانِ عَلِمَ أَن سَيَكُونُ مِنكُم مَّرْضَىٰ وَءَاخَرُونَ
يَضْرِبُونَ فِي ٱلْأَرْضِ يَبْتَغُونَ مِن فَضْلِ ٱللَّهِ وَءَاخَرُونَ يُقَـٰتِلُونَ فِي سَبِيلِ
ٱللَّهِ فَٱقْرَءُوا مَا تَيَسَّرَ مِنْهُ وَأَقِيمُوا ٱلصَّلَوٰةَ وَءَاتُوا ٱلزَّكَوٰةَ وَأَقْرِضُوا ٱللَّهَ
قَرْضًا حَسَنًا وَمَا تُقَدِّمُوا لِأَنفُسِكُم مِّنْ خَيْرٍ تَجِدُوهُ عِندَ ٱللَّهِ هُوَ خَيْرًا وَأَعْظَمَ أَجْرًا
وَٱسْتَغْفِرُوا ٱللَّهَ إِنَّ ٱللَّهَ غَفُورٌ رَّحِيمٌ ۝

Muslim and Bukhari narrated another report from Asma, in which she said: "There was a solar eclipse at the time of the Prophet (peace and blessings be upon him). I saw the Messenger of Allāh (peace and blessings be upon him) standing (in prayer), so I joined him. The Prophet was standing for so long that I felt I tired, but then I noticed an old woman who was tired and weak, then I said to myself: The woman looks much weaker than I, so I must continue to stand. Then the Prophet (peace be upon him) bowed, and again remained in that position for a long time; then the Prophet (peace be upon him) raised his head and stood for a long time. So if anyone entered the Masjid at this point they might think that the Prophet had not yet bowed in ruku. The Prophet then completed the prayer when the eclipse was over. He addressed the people, praising and glorifying Allāh the Almighty."

During that golden era, the time of the Prophet (peace and blessings be upon him), women knew about their own religion and were aware about the affairs that concerned the Muslims in this world and the next. When women heard the call to prayer, they rushed to the masjid to hear the Prophet (peace and blessings be upon him).

Fatimah bint Qays, one of the earliest migrant women (muhajirat), said: "The prayer was called, so I hurried with the others to the masjid, and prayed with the Messenger of Allāh (peace and blessings be upon him). I was in the first row for women, which was just behind the last row of men."

Some people tend to believe that woman at the back row in prayer, behind the last row of men, means that women are lower and less deserving and men have power. This is not correct. The reason is that: (i) Men are not disciplined often, and (ii) Women are far more disciplined.

If you think about it, when we were children in school, the disciplined students would often sit in the back of the classroom, while those children who were a bit rowdy, the teacher would sit them in the front.

Initially, at the Masjid al-Nabawi, both men and women entered the masjid through the same door. When this caused overcrowding on entrances and exits, the Messenger of Allāh (peace and blessings be upon him) said: "It would be better if this door of the Masjid is left for women." Upon this, the door became known up until today as: "The Women's Door" or Bab al-Nisa.

It is very clear, from many sahih reports, that women went to the masjid on various occasions and that this attendance was an approved custom at the time of the Prophet (peace and blessings be upon him). Even when a woman was attacked once on her way to the masjid, this incident did not make the Prophet (peace and blessings be upon him) have any reservations about allowing women to go to the masjid.

The Prophet still allowed women to do what made them happy, and prohibited men preventing them, because there is so much benefit, spiritual, knowledge, mental, and otherwise, for women in attending prayers and lectures at the masjid. Wail al-Kindi reported that a good woman was once attacked by a man in the early morning, while she was on her way to the masjid for Fajr prayer. The woman shouted to a passer-by for help, then a large group of men ran to her. Instead they seized the man to whom she had first called for help, so her attacker ran away. They brought the innocent man to her, and he said:

"But I am the one who answered your call for help; your attacker got away."

They brought the man to the Messenger of Allāh (peace and blessings be upon him), and told him that this man had attacked the woman. However, the man said: "I was the one who answered her call for help against her attacker, but these people seized me and brought me here." The woman said: "He is lying; he is the one who attacked me."

The Messenger of Allāh (peace be upon him) said: "Take him away and stone him." But then another man stood up and said, "Please do not stone him, stone me instead, for I am the one who attacked the woman."

Now the Messenger of Allāh (peace and blessings be upon him) had three people before him: the man who had attacked the woman, the man who had answered her calls for help, and the woman.

The Prophet (peace and blessings be upon him) told the attacker: "As for you, Allāh has forgiven you for your honesty," and the Prophet spoke kind words to the one who had helped the woman. Then Omar said: "Stone the one who has admitted to the crime of adultery."

But the Prophet (peace be upon him) said: "No, for he has repented to Allāh by speaking the truth, saving this man's life, and asking to be stoned instead. His act of repentance and truthfulness was so great that if the people were to repent in this manner always, it would be accepted from them."

The Messenger of Allāh (peace and blessings be upon him) appreciated the circumstances of the women that attended the congregational prayers, so he was kind to the women, and he would always shorten the prayer if he heard a child crying, so that the mother would never become distressed and tired.

Many Sahih reports describe how the Prophet (peace and blessings be upon him) used to organize women at congregational prayers, for example: "The best row for men is the front, and the worst is the back row; the best row for women is at the back, and the worst row is at the front." Another hadith report, deals with allowing women to leave the masjid before the men, after the prayer is over.

Hind bint al-Harith said that Umm Salamah, the wife of the Prophet (peace and blessings be upon him), told her that when the obligatory prayer was over, women before the men would get up to leave.

The Messenger of Allāh (peace and blessings be upon him) and the men would wait as long as Allāh willed. When the Prophet (peace and blessings be upon him) got up to leave, the men would only then get up to leave.

Muslim and Bukhari also reported a hadith concerning how a woman can draw the Imam's attention to something during the prayer by clapping. Sahl ibn Sa'd al-Sa'idi said: "The Messenger of Allāh (peace and blessings be upon him) said: 'Why do I see you clapping so much?

Whoever notices any error in my prayer should say 'Subhan Allāh,' for by doing so he will alert me to the error. Clapping is only for women.'"

The number of women that attended the masjid increased daily until, at the time of the Abbasids, the women filled the courtyard of the masjid, and men would have no choice but to pray behind them. This was the verdict (fatwa) of Imam Malik, Ibn al-Qasim said: "I asked Imam Malik about the men who come to the masjid and found the courtyard filled with women, and the masjid itself filled with men. May those men pray behind the women?" Malik said: 'Yes their prayer is valid.'"

However, women going out to the masjid must be careful not a cause fitnah (temptations). Men and women must always behave in accordance with the Prophet's teachings of purity of thought and behavior. If for any reason there is the fear of temptations, then it is best for women to pray at home. This is what is indicated by the hadith of the Prophet (peace and blessings be upon him): "Do not stop your women from going to the masjid, although their houses are better for them."

However, some men feared the possibility of fitnah, and so they took this as an excuse to prohibit their women from going to the masjid. So the Prophet (peace and blessings be upon him) said: "Do not prevent the women from going to the masjid at night." One of the sons of Abdullah ibn Omar said: "We will not let women go out because it will give rise to deviation and suspicion." Ibn Omar scolded him and said: "the Messenger of Allāh (peace be upon him) said such-and-such and you say: 'No, we will not let them!'"

It is also permissible for women to attend the gatherings of the Muslims in the masjid. There is a lot to be gained from this. However, certain conditions apply to this permission. The most important of which is that women who go to the masjid must not wear perfume or make-up. Zaynab al-Thaqafiyyah said that the Prophet (peace and blessings be upon him) said: "If any woman want to attend Isha prayer, they she should not wear perfume."

O Prophet, say to your wives, "If you should desire the worldly life and its adornment, then come, I will provide for you and give you a gracious release. (33:28)

يَـٰٓأَيُّهَا ٱلنَّبِىُّ قُل لِّأَزْوَٰجِكَ إِن كُنتُنَّ تُرِدْنَ ٱلْحَيَوٰةَ ٱلدُّنْيَا وَزِينَتَهَا فَتَعَالَيْنَ أُمَتِّعْكُنَّ وَأُسَرِّحْكُنَّ سَرَاحًا جَمِيلًا ﴿٢٨﴾

Whoever turns away from My remembrance - indeed, he will have a depressed life, and We will gather him on the Day of Resurrection blind." (20:124)

$$\text{وَمَنْ أَعْرَضَ عَن ذِكْرِى فَإِنَّ لَهُ مَعِيشَةً ضَنكًا وَنَحْشُرُهُ يَوْمَ الْقِيَـٰمَةِ أَعْمَىٰ ﴿١٢٤﴾}$$

Or [the state of a disbeliever] is like the darkness in a vast deep sea, overwhelmed with a great wave topped by a great wave, topped by dark clouds, darkness, one above another, if a man stretches out his hand, he can hardly see it! And he for whom Allah has not appointed light, for him there is no light. (24:40)

$$\text{أَوْ كَظُلُمَـٰتٍ فِى بَحْرٍ لُّجِّىٍّ يَغْشَىٰهُ مَوْجٌ مِّن فَوْقِهِ مَوْجٌ مِّن فَوْقِهِ سَحَابٌ ظُلُمَـٰتٌ بَعْضُهَا فَوْقَ بَعْضٍ إِذَآ أَخْرَجَ يَدَهُ لَمْ يَكَدْ يَرَىٰهَا وَمَن لَّمْ يَجْعَلِ اللَّهُ لَهُ نُورًا فَمَا لَهُ مِن نُّورٍ ﴿٤٠﴾}$$

Allah, the Merciful, answers the prayer of the disbeliever who is in distress; so how much more can a good Muslim woman expect who never associates partners with Allah?

It is He who enables you to travel on land and sea until, when you are in ships and they sail with them by a good wind and they rejoice therein, there comes a storm wind and the waves come upon them from everywhere and they assume that they are surrounded, supplicating Allah, sincere to Him in religion, "If You should save us from this, we will surely be among the thankful." (10:22)

هُوَ الَّذِى يُسَيِّرُكُمْ فِي الْبَرِّ وَالْبَحْرِ حَتَّى إِذَا كُنتُمْ فِي الْفُلْكِ وَجَرَيْنَ بِهِم بِرِيحٍ طَيِّبَةٍ وَفَرِحُوا بِهَا جَاءَتْهَا رِيحٌ عَاصِفٌ وَجَاءَهُمُ الْمَوْجُ مِن كُلِّ مَكَانٍ وَظَنُّوا أَنَّهُمْ أُحِيطَ بِهِمْ دَعَوُا اللَّهَ مُخْلِصِينَ لَهُ الدِّينَ لَئِنْ أَنجَيْتَنَا مِنْ هَذِهِ لَنَكُونَنَّ مِنَ الشَّاكِرِينَ ﴿٢٢﴾

The Messenger of Allah (peace and blessings be upon him) said: We do not say other than that which pleases Allah. Upon you is a sacred duty to submit yourself to what is preordained for you. If you fulfill this duty, you will be successful in the long run. Your only escape is to believe in preordainment, since whatever has been written must inevitably take place. No artifice or subterfuge can protect you from it.

Women may Attend Eid Prayers

Allāh has honored all women and made them equal with man as to obligatory acts of worship. Women are encouraged to join public gatherings on Eid al-Adha and Eid al-Fitr, so that they may take part in these blessed prayers. This is also confirmed in a number of Hadith reported by Bukhari and Muslim, in which we see that the Prophet (peace and blessings be upon him) taught that all the women should come to these occasions. He said that even menstruating women should attend and take part in these blessed and joyous occasions. Women must try to keep away from the prayer-place itself until the menstruation period is over. His concern that all women should attend the prayers was so great that he said that all women who had more than one jilbab (outer garment), should give a garment to her sister or neighbor who had none. In this way he encouraged all women to attend Eid prayers and to do good and righteous deeds.

One day a good woman went to visit her sister at the castle of Banu Khalaf, and she narrated something from her sister. The sister's husband took part in a military campaigns with the Prophet (peace and blessings be upon him), and her sister also had accompanied her husband. The sister said: "We took care of the wounded." Her sister asked the Messenger of Allāh (peace and blessings be upon him): "If a woman does not have a jilbaband (robe), then she cannot go to the Masjid?" He (peace be upon him) said: "Let her friend or sister give her one of her jilbabs, so that she can come out and join the righteous gatherings."

Jabir ibn Abdullah said: "The Messenger of Allāh (peace and blessings be upon him) led the prayer during Eid al-Fitr. Then he addressed the people. When the Prophet of Allāh (peace and blessings be upon him) had finished his khutbah (sermon), he spoke to women, and then Bilal spread out his cloak for the women to put their sadaqah (donation) in it. Ibn Jurayj asked: "Was it zakat al-fitr?" He said: "No, it was the sadaqah."

So a woman threw her ring into the cloak, then others did the same. According to this hadith, the Messenger of Allāh (peace and blessings be upon him) accepted the sadaqah that they themselves willingly gave. This is shows the importance of congregational prayer for both men and women.

Although Islam does not force women to attend congregational prayer, women should still gather together at home, and offer the prayers in congregation. In this case, the woman who is leading the prayer must stand in the middle of the (first) row, not in front. The women do not have to recite the adhan or the iqamah. This is what Umm Salamah, the wife of the Prophet (peace be upon him), did when she led women in prayer.

Your life is the product of your actions and thoughts. Those actions and thoughts that you invest in will have a great effect upon your life, regardless of whether they are good actions and thoughts or bad.

Worshiping Allah alone leads to happiness. In an authentic hadith, the Prophet (peace and blessings be upon him) said: "Verily, Allah will say to His slave as He is taking account of him on the Day of Judgment: 'O'son of Adam, I was hungry and you did not feed Me.' He will answer: "How can I feed You and You are the Lord of the worlds!' He will say: 'Did you not know that My slave so and so who is the son of so and so felt hunger, and you did not feed him. Alas! Had you fed him you would have found that reward with Me. O'son of Adam, I was thirsty and you gave Me nothing to drink.' He will say: 'How can I give You water, and You are the Lord of the worlds!' He will say: 'Did you not know that My slave so and so, the son of so and so felt thirsty and you did not give him water to drink. Alas! If you had given him, you would have found that reward with Me. O'son of Adam, I became ill and you did not visit Me.' He will say: 'How can I visit You and You are the Lord of the worlds!' He will say: 'Did you not know that My slave so and so, the son of so and so became ill and you did not visit him. Alas! Had you visited him, you would have found <u>Me</u> with him.'"

Allah, the Merciful, is with those whose hearts are sad and troubled, as is the case with the person who is ill. And in another hadith, the Prophet, peace be upon him, said: "There is reward in each moist liver (i.e. to do service to any living creature will be rewarded)."

Allah admitted a prostitute from the children of Israel into Paradise because she gave a drink to a dog that was very thirsty. So what will be the case for the one who feeds other humans, giving them some water and removing from them hardships!

In an authentic hadith, the Prophet, peace be upon him said: "Whoever has extra provision should give from it to the one who has no provision. And whoever has an extra mount (i.e. donkey, horse, and camel) should give with this extra to the one who has no mount."

Women should try to Pray Sunnah and Nafil Prayer

Women must not limit themselves to the five daily obligatory prayers; they must try to pray Sunnah prayers as the Prophet (peace and blessings be upon him) did, and women must try to pray many of the nafil (supererogatory) prayers as their time and energy allow.

And keep constant vigil with it (The Qur'an) (part) of the night (These are the late night supererogatory prayers) as an accordance for you; it may be that your Lord will make you rise again to a praised station. (17:79)

وَمِنَ ٱلَّيْلِ فَتَهَجَّدْ بِهِۦ نَافِلَةً لَّكَ عَسَىٰٓ أَن يَبْعَثَكَ رَبُّكَ مَقَامًا مَّحْمُودًا ﴿٧٩﴾

These prayers are salat al-duha, and Sunnah prayers following Maghrib, Isha, and prayers offered at night. Nafil prayers bring a person closer to God (Allāh), and can earn them the love of Allāh. There is no clearer words of the great status attained by a person who draws closer to Allāh by praying nafil. On the authority of Abu Hurayrah (may Allāh be pleased with him), who said that the Messenger of Allāh (peace and blessing be upon him) said: Allāh (mighty and sublime be He) said: Whosoever shows enmity to someone faithful, I shall be at war with him. When I love someone I am his hearing with which he hears, his seeing with which he sees, his hand with which he strikes and his foot with which he walks. And when My servants ask you, [O Muhammad], concerning Me - indeed I am near. I respond to the invocation of the supplicant when he calls upon Me. So let them respond to Me [by obedience] and believe in Me that they may be [rightly] guided. (2:186)

وَإِذَا سَأَلَكَ عِبَادِى عَنِّى فَإِنِّى قَرِيبٌ أُجِيبُ دَعْوَةَ ٱلدَّاعِ إِذَا دَعَانِ فَلْيَسْتَجِيبُوا لِى وَلْيُؤْمِنُوا بِى لَعَلَّهُمْ يَرْشُدُونَ ﴿١٨٦﴾

Every love that leads away from Allah in fact a punishment, and only a love that leads to Allah is a heartfelt and pure love. She who keeps her heart near Allah will find peace and tranquility, whilst she who gives her heart to the people will find restlessness and apprehension. For everything that a slave loses there is a substitute, but the one who loses Allah will never find anything to replace Him.

When Allāh loves a slave, calls out the Angel Jibril and says: "I love so-and-so; so love that person." Then the Angel Jibril loves that person. After that, the Angel announces to the inhabitants of heavens that Allāh loves that person; and so the inhabitants of the heavens also love him and then make people on earth love them too. Allāh loves those who are constantly repentant and loves those who purify themselves. (2:222)

The Prophet (peace be upon him) used to pray a lot at night that his feet became swollen often. Aishah (May Allāh be pleased with her) asked him: "Why do you do this, Messenger of Allāh, when Allāh has forgiven your sins, past and future?" He (peace and blessings be upon him) said: "Should I not be a grateful servant?"

The Prophet's wife Zaynab (May Allāh be pleased with her) used to pray nafil prayers, and her prayers were long. One day she put up a rope between two column posts in the masjid, so that when she was tired, she can lean against the rope for a while. When the Messenger of Allāh (peace be upon him) entered the masjid and saw the rope, he asked: "What is this the reason for the rope?"

The people answered: "It belongs to Zaynab. When she feels tired, she leans against the rope." He (peace be upon him) said: "Please untie the rope; let any of you pray as long as he/she has the energy, and if you feel tired, then please sit down."

A woman of Banu Asad, al-Hawla bint (daughter of) Tuwayt, used to pray all night, and she hardly ever slept. One day she visited Aishah when the Prophet (peace be upon him) was present. Aishah told him: "This is al-Hawla' bint Tuwayt. They say that she never sleeps at night." The Messenger of Allāh (peace and blessings be upon him) said: "Please do only as much as you can, for by Allāh, Allāh never gets tired, but humans do."

The virtue of a deed that is done persistently, whether it be Qiyam al-Lail or anything else. The command to be moderate in worship, which means adopting what one can persist in. The command to the one who gets tired or weary when praying to stop until that feeling passes. Aishah reported that the Messenger of Allāh (peace be upon him) had a mat and he used it for making an apartment during the night and observed prayer in it, and the people began to pray with him, and he spread it (the mat) during the day time. The people crowded round him one night.

He (the Holy Prophet) then said: O people, perform such acts as you are capable of doing, for Allāh does not grow weary but you will get tired. The acts most pleasing to Allāh are those which are done continuously, even if they are small. And it was the habit of the members of Muhammad's (peace be upon him) household that whenever they did an act they did it continuously.

If Allah wishes good for one of His slaves, He will cover him with slumber as a security, as occurred to Talha (may Allah be pleased with him) before the battle of Uhud. A short time before the battle, while the disbelievers waited in nervous fear, Allah covered him with a slumber that made him, on a few occasions, drop his sword, so serene and calm did he feel. Allah, the Almighty, said: Say, "Do you await for us except one of the two best things while we await for you that Allah will afflict you with punishment from Himself or at our hands? So wait; indeed we, along with you, are waiting." (9:52)

قُلْ هَلْ تَرَبَّصُونَ بِنَآ إِلَّا إِحْدَى الْحُسْنَيَيْنِ وَنَحْنُ نَتَرَبَّصُ
بِكُمْ أَن يُصِيبَكُمُ اللَّهُ بِعَذَابٍ مِّنْ عِندِهِ أَوْ بِأَيْدِينَا
فَتَرَبَّصُوٓا إِنَّا مَعَكُم مُّتَرَبِّصُونَ ۝

And it is not [possible] for one to die except by permission of Allah at a decree determined. And whoever desires the reward of this world - We will give him thereof; and whoever desires the reward of the Hereafter - We will give him thereof. And we will reward the grateful. (3:145)

وَمَا كَانَ لِنَفْسٍ أَن تَمُوتَ إِلَّا بِإِذْنِ اللَّهِ كِتَـٰبًا مُّؤَجَّلًا وَمَن
يُرِدْ ثَوَابَ الدُّنْيَا نُؤْتِهِ مِنْهَا وَمَن يُرِدْ ثَوَابَ الْآخِرَةِ نُؤْتِهِ مِنْهَا
وَسَنَجْزِى الشَّـٰكِرِينَ ۝

Ali (may Allah be pleased with him) said: "Which of the two days of death do I fear? The day in which it was not decreed for me to die or the day in which death was preordained for me. As for the former, I fear it not. And as for the latter, it is destined to happen, and even cautious ones cannot be saved on that day."

Abu Bakr (may Allah be pleased with him) said: "Seek out death (i.e. be brave) and you shall be granted life."

Allah will always defend you and His angels ask forgiveness for you; the believers share with you their supplications in every prayer; the Prophet, peace and blessings be upon him, will intercede for the believers; the Quran is filled with good promises; and above all is the mercy of He Who is the Most Merciful.

Your good deed is increased so that its value is multiplied tenfold or seven hundred fold or even much, much more.

Allah is kind and Merciful. The evil deed is valued without increase or multiplication, and your Allah can forgive even that. How often do we see Allah's mercy and generosity, generosity that is unmatched by any! And benevolence from anyone else cannot reach even near His Benevolence.

Perform Prayers Properly

One of the most beneficial of remedies is persisting in prayer and du'a. And you must perform your prayers properly, with deep concentration and precision. Think of the ayat (Quran) while reciting them, and the words of praise and glorification of Allāh. If you wish to check how much you love Allah, then see how much your heart loves the Quran, and you will know the answer. Your soul should be flooded with fear of Allāh, and with gratitude. If the devil happens to whisper something to you during the prayer, to distract you, try to focus more on the words that you are reciting from the Quran.

Do not rush back to your work when you finished praying. Rather, as the Prophet (peace be upon her) used to do, ask Allāh for forgiveness by saying "Astaghfir-Allāh" three times, and try to repeat the following dua:

Allāhumma anta al-salam, Wa minka al-salam, Tabaraka ya dha'l-jalali wa'l-ikram

(O Allāh, You are Peace and from You comes peace, Blessed are You, O Lord of majesty and honor.)

Then repeat the adhkar and dua's that the Prophet (peace be upon him) used to recite after completing his prayer. There are many such adhkar, one of the most important of which is to repeat "*Subhan Allāh*" 33 times, *La ilaha ill-Allāh*" 33 times, "*Allāhu akbar* 33 times, then to complete one hundred with *La illaha ill-Allāh wahdahu la shaika lah, lahu'l-mulk wa lahu'l-hamd, wa huwa `ala kulli shayin qadir.*

According to a Sahih hadith, the Prophet (peace and blessings be upon him) said: Whoever glorifies Allāh (SWT) (says *subhan Allāh*) after every prayer 33 times, praises Allāh (says *al-hamdu lillah*) 33 times, and magnifies Allāh (says *Allāhu akbar) 33 times,* which adds up to 99, then completes one hundred by saying *La illaha ill-Allāh wahdahu la shaika lah, lahu'l-mulk wa lahu'l-hamd, wa huwa `ala kulli shayin qadir*, their sins will be forgiven, even if they were as much as the sand of the earth.

Then she turns to Allāh humbly asking Him to correct all her affairs, in this world and the next one, and to bless her abundantly and to guide her in everything.

Hold old firmly to the rope of Allāh all together and do not become divided. And remember the favor of Allāh upon you - when you were enemies and He brought your hearts together and you became, by His favor, brothers. And you were on the edge of a pit of the Fire, and He saved you from it. Thus does Allāh make clear to you His verses that you may be guided. (3:103)

وَٱعْتَصِمُوا بِحَبْلِ ٱللَّهِ جَمِيعًا وَلَا تَفَرَّقُوا وَٱذْكُرُوا نِعْمَتَ ٱللَّهِ عَلَيْكُمْ إِذْ كُنتُمْ أَعْدَآءً فَأَلَّفَ بَيْنَ قُلُوبِكُمْ فَأَصْبَحْتُم بِنِعْمَتِهِۦٓ إِخْوَٰنًا وَكُنتُمْ عَلَىٰ شَفَا حُفْرَةٍ مِّنَ ٱلنَّارِ فَأَنقَذَكُم مِّنْهَا كَذَٰلِكَ يُبَيِّنُ ٱللَّهُ لَكُمْ ءَايَٰتِهِۦ لَعَلَّكُمْ تَهْتَدُونَ ﴿١٠٣﴾

The righteous woman finishes her prayers, purified in her heart. Allāh will help her to cope with the burdens of life. Allāh will make sure that she is not afraid nor sad. And Allāh will guide her not to be miserly if she receives good fortune. People are often very impatient; they get upset when evil touches them; and they become very stingy when good fortune reaches them. And they become not so those devoted to Prayer. Patience is the key. The heart must never feel anger towards that which is destined. And beware of preoccupying your heart with what it has not been created for.

If your heart is fed by love and faith, the greed for things and pleasure would disappear. Sitting with the poor and less fortunate people removes the ego and pride from your heart. And those in whose wealth is a recognized right for the poor who asks and them who is prevented [for some reason from asking]) (70:19-25)

﴿ إِنَّ ٱلْإِنسَٰنَ خُلِقَ هَلُوعًا ١٩

إِذَا مَسَّهُ ٱلشَّرُّ جَزُوعًا ٢٠

وَإِذَا مَسَّهُ ٱلْخَيْرُ مَنُوعًا ٢١

إِلَّا ٱلْمُصَلِّينَ ٢٢

ٱلَّذِينَ هُمْ عَلَىٰ صَلَاتِهِمْ دَآئِمُونَ ٢٣

وَٱلَّذِينَ فِىٓ أَمْوَٰلِهِمْ حَقٌّ مَّعْلُومٌ ٢٤

لِّلسَّآئِلِ وَٱلْمَحْرُومِ ٢٥

When there is money in your hand and not in your heart, it will not harm you even if it is a lot; and when it is in your heart, it will harm you even if there is none in your hands.

When a person spends his entire day with no concern but Allah alone, Allah will take care of all his needs and take care of all that is worrying him; He will empty his heart so that it will be filled only with love for Him.

If you do not associate partners with Allah, if you believe in the true religion, and if you love Allah and His Messenger, peace and blessings be upon him, do not feel sad. If you feel regret for your bad deeds and you rejoice when you do a worthy act, do not feel sad. You have much good with you that you do not perceive.

If you are able to establish the state of balanced harmony that is referred to in the following hadith, do not feel bad: "How wonderful is the state of the believer. All of his affairs are good for him! And that is not so, except for the believer. If he has cause to be happy, he is thankful, and that is good for him. And if he is afflicted with hardship, he is patient, and that is good for him."

Do not be bad: forbearance in times of distress
is the path to both success and happiness. And
be patient, [O Muhammad], and your patience
is not but through Allah. And do not grieve
over them and do not be in distress over what
they conspire. (16: 127)

وَٱصۡبِرۡ وَمَا صَبۡرُكَ إِلَّا بِٱللَّهِۚ وَلَا تَحۡزَنۡ عَلَيۡهِمۡ وَلَا تَكُ فِى ضَيۡقٖ مِّمَّا يَمۡكُرُونَ ﴿١٢٧﴾

Therefore do thou hold Patience,- a Patience
of beautiful (contentment). (70:5)

فَٱصۡبِرۡ صَبۡرٗا جَمِيلًا ﴿٥﴾

And they brought upon his shirt false blood.
[Jacob] said, "Rather, your souls have enticed
you to something, so patience is most fitting.
And Allah is the one sought for help against
that which you describe." (12:18)

وَجَآءُو عَلَىٰ قَمِيصِهِۦ بِدَمٖ كَذِبٖۚ قَالَ بَلۡ سَوَّلَتۡ لَكُمۡ أَنفُسُكُمۡ أَمۡرٗاۖ فَصَبۡرٞ جَمِيلٞۖ وَٱللَّهُ ٱلۡمُسۡتَعَانُ عَلَىٰ مَا تَصِفُونَ ﴿١٨﴾

Peace be upon you for what you patiently endured. And excellent is the final home. (13:24)

سَلَٰمٌ عَلَيْكُم بِمَا صَبَرْتُمْ فَنِعْمَ عُقْبَى ٱلدَّارِ ﴿٢٤﴾

O my son, establish prayer, enjoin what is right, forbid what is wrong, and be patient over what befalls you. Indeed, [all] that is of the matters [requiring] determination. (31:17)

يَٰبُنَىَّ أَقِمِ ٱلصَّلَوٰةَ وَأْمُرْ بِٱلْمَعْرُوفِ وَٱنْهَ عَنِ ٱلْمُنكَرِ وَٱصْبِرْ عَلَىٰ مَآ أَصَابَكَ إِنَّ ذَٰلِكَ مِنْ عَزْمِ ٱلْأُمُورِ ﴿١٧﴾

O you who have believed, persevere and endure and remain stationed and fear Allah that you may be successful. (3:200)

يَٰأَيُّهَا ٱلَّذِينَ ءَامَنُوا ٱصْبِرُوا وَصَابِرُوا وَرَابِطُوا وَٱتَّقُوا ٱللَّهَ لَعَلَّكُمْ تُفْلِحُونَ ﴿٢٠٠﴾

Omar (may Allah be pleased with him) said: "Through patience we have now achieved a good life."

For the people of the Sunnah, there are three things that they resort to when faced with calamity: prayer, patience, and waiting with expectation for a good outcome.

Muslim once said: "We have poured them a glass and they have similarly poured one for us (alluding to the blood enemies draw from each other in battle). But in the face of death, we were the more patient."

In an authentic hadith, the Prophet, peace and blessings be upon him, said: "There is none who is more patient when he hears something offensive than Allah. They claim that He has a child and a wife, yet He gives them health and provisions."

The Prophet, peace and blessings be upon him, also said: "May Allah have mercy on Moses. He was tested with more than this (i.e. than what I have been tested with), and he was still patient."

And the Prophet, peace and blessings be upon him, said: "Whoever is patient, Allah will give him further strength to continue to be patient."

Muslim once said: "I have crawled my way to distinction, and those who have struggled have reached it. With the toil of labor, and the sparing of no small effort, many have tried to reach it, and most became tired or bored trying. And they embrace distinction that remain true and are patient. Do not consider distinction to be an apple that you eat. You will not achieve distinction until you beat hardship and pain with your patience."

Righteous women must pay zakat on their wealth

If a person were given all of the world and what is in it, it would not fill their emptiness. A good woman pays zakat (charity). Each year at a specified time, women must estimate how much they own and must pay it. Zakat is not just charity. It is a pillar of Islam, and there is no compromise or excuse when it comes to helping the needy and poor, even if you must pay thousands or even millions of dollars. The words of Abu Bakr (May Allāh have mercy on him) concerning the people who refused to pay their zakat echo down the centuries to us: "By Allāh I will fight whoever separates salat and zakat."

No woman can claim to be exempted because she is a woman. In Islam and in the eyes of Allāh, women and men are equal. And they must pray and fast the same.

Charity brings peace to the giver. Among the factors that contribute to one's happiness are performing acts of kindness to others and giving charity.

O you who have believed, spend from that which We have provided for you before there comes a Day in which there is no exchange and no friendship and no intercession. And the disbelievers - they are the wrongdoers. (2:254)

يَٰٓأَيُّهَا ٱلَّذِينَ ءَامَنُوٓاْ أَنفِقُواْ مِمَّا رَزَقْنَٰكُم مِّن قَبْلِ أَن يَأْتِىَ يَوْمٌ لَّا بَيْعٌ فِيهِ وَلَا خُلَّةٌ وَلَا شَفَٰعَةٌ وَٱلْكَٰفِرُونَ هُمُ ٱلظَّٰلِمُونَ ﴿٢٥٤﴾

Indeed, the Muslim men and Muslim women, the believing men and believing women, the obedient men and obedient women, the truthful men and truthful women, the patient men and patient women, the humble men and humble women, the charitable men and charitable women, the fasting men and fasting women, the men who guard their private parts and the women who do so, and the men who remember Allah often and the women who do so - for them Allah has prepared forgiveness and a great reward. (33:35)

إِنَّ ٱلْمُسْلِمِينَ وَٱلْمُسْلِمَٰتِ وَٱلْمُؤْمِنِينَ وَٱلْمُؤْمِنَٰتِ وَٱلْقَٰنِتِينَ وَٱلْقَٰنِتَٰتِ وَٱلصَّٰدِقِينَ وَٱلصَّٰدِقَٰتِ وَٱلصَّٰبِرِينَ وَٱلصَّٰبِرَٰتِ وَٱلْخَٰشِعِينَ وَٱلْخَٰشِعَٰتِ وَٱلْمُتَصَدِّقِينَ وَٱلْمُتَصَدِّقَٰتِ وَٱلصَّٰٓئِمِينَ وَٱلصَّٰٓئِمَٰتِ وَٱلْحَٰفِظِينَ فُرُوجَهُمْ وَٱلْحَٰفِظَٰتِ وَٱلذَّٰكِرِينَ ٱللَّهَ كَثِيرًا وَٱلذَّٰكِرَٰتِ أَعَدَّ ٱللَّهُ لَهُم مَّغْفِرَةً وَأَجْرًا عَظِيمًا ﴿٣٥﴾

And the example of those who spend their wealth seeking means to the approval of Allah and assuring [reward for] themselves is like a garden on high ground which is hit by a downpour - so it yields its fruits in double. And [even] if it is not hit by a downpour, then a drizzle [is sufficient]. And Allah, of what you do, is Seeing. (2:265)

وَمَثَلُ ٱلَّذِينَ يُنفِقُونَ أَمْوَالَهُمُ ٱبْتِغَآءَ مَرْضَاتِ ٱللَّهِ وَتَثْبِيتًا مِّنْ أَنفُسِهِمْ كَمَثَلِ جَنَّةٍ بِرَبْوَةٍ أَصَابَهَا وَابِلٌ فَـَٔاتَتْ أُكُلَهَا ضِعْفَيْنِ فَإِن لَّمْ يُصِبْهَا وَابِلٌ فَطَلٌّ ۗ وَٱللَّهُ بِمَا تَعْمَلُونَ بَصِيرٌ ﴿٢٦٥﴾

And do not make your hand [as] chained to
your neck or extend it completely and [thereby]
become blamed and insolvent. (17:29)

وَلَا تَجْعَلْ يَدَكَ مَغْلُولَةً إِلَىٰ عُنُقِكَ وَلَا تَبْسُطْهَا كُلَّ ٱلْبَسْطِ فَتَقْعُدَ مَلُومًا مَّحْسُورًا ﴿٢٩﴾

Miserly people are deplorable in their manners
and are always ill at ease. They are stingy in
sharing the favors of Allah. If the miser only
knew that he would achieve happiness by
spending money on those who are poor, then
he would surely race to give charity.

If you loan Allah a goodly loan, He will multiply it for you and forgive you. And Allah is Most Appreciative and Forbearing. (64:17)

And [also for] those who were settled in al-Madinah and [adopted] the faith before them. They love those who emigrated to them and find not any want in their breasts of what the emigrants were given but give [them] preference over themselves, even though they are in privation. And whoever is protected from the stinginess of his soul - it is those who will be the successful. (59:9)

وَٱلَّذِينَ تَبَوَّءُو ٱلدَّارَ وَٱلْإِيمَٰنَ مِن قَبْلِهِمْ يُحِبُّونَ مَنْ هَاجَرَ إِلَيْهِمْ وَلَا يَجِدُونَ فِى صُدُورِهِمْ حَاجَةً مِّمَّآ أُوتُواْ وَيُؤْثِرُونَ عَلَىٰٓ أَنفُسِهِمْ وَلَوْ كَانَ بِهِمْ خَصَاصَةٌ وَمَن يُوقَ شُحَّ نَفْسِهِۦ فَأُوْلَٰٓئِكَ هُمُ ٱلْمُفْلِحُونَ ﴿٩﴾

A man once said to his wife: "If you have prepared a meal, invite a hungry person, for I cannot bear to eat by myself." Then he said to her, proclaiming his philosophy:

"Name a very generous woman or man who died from being generous, or a miserly woman or man who lived forever, and I will desist."

<u>Righteous women fast during the day and pray as men do</u>

Be to Allah as He wishes, and He will be to you more than you can wish for. Righteous women fast the month of Ramadan, and their soul is always filled with faith. O you who have believed, decreed upon you is fasting as it was decreed upon those before you that you may become righteous. (2:183)

يَٰٓأَيُّهَا ٱلَّذِينَ ءَامَنُوا۟ كُتِبَ عَلَيْكُمُ ٱلصِّيَامُ كَمَا كُتِبَ عَلَى ٱلَّذِينَ مِن قَبْلِكُمْ لَعَلَّكُمْ تَتَّقُونَ ﴿١٨٣﴾

Whoever fasts Ramadan out of faith and hope of reward, all their previous sins will be forgiven. So you should have the attitude of one who truly fasts, whose eyes and ears keep away from all kinds of sins that may diminish the reward.

If a person finds themselves exposed to the trials of argument, then simply follows the Prophet's advice: "Speech remains as a slave to you, but the moment it leaves your mouth, you become its slave."

When any of you is fasting, do not utter foul words and do not raise your voice in anger. If someone provokes you, just say, 'I am fasting as Allāh commanded me. Whoever does not give up evil actions and false speech, then Allāh has no need of them giving up water and food.

The reward for every good deed Allāh will multiply between 10 and 700 times. However, fasting is different. Only Allāh knows if you are truly fasting or not. Allāh said: "Except for fasting, because it is for Me and I Myself will give payment for it." Then for everyone who fast, there are two * times of joy, at sunset when one eats, and one when they meet Allāh.

Allāh told Prophet Moses (peace be upon him), the smell that comes from the mouth of one who is fasting is more pleasing to Me than the scent of musk.

The Prophet (peace be upon him) did more good deeds during Ramadan than at other times, especially during the last 10 days. Aishah (May Allāh be pleased with her) said: "When the last 10 days of Ramadan began, the Messenger of Allāh (peace be upon him) stayed up all nights and abstained from marital relations."

The Prophet (peace be upon him) asked Muslims to seek laylat al-qadr, and asked them to try to spend that night in prayer: "Seek laylat al-qadr during the last 10 days of Ramadan. Whoever worships Allāh out of faith and hope of reward, all his previous sins will be forgiven."

The good woman helps her family to get up to eat suhur, in obedience to the command of the Prophet (peace be upon him). This is what the Prophet (peace be upon him) used to do and he taught his Companions too.

You must always contemplate the many forms of worship that are legislated in Islam. There are deeds of the heart, of the tongue, of the limbs, and of wealth - by spending it for a good cause. The prayer, alms giving, fasting, pilgrimages to Makkah, fighting in the way of Allah, these are only some good examples of worship. The prayer as learning involves some memorization. The prayer involves standing, bowing, prostrating, and sitting. If you desire relaxation, vitality, and continued productivity, then bring diversity into your life, your reading, and your daily work. In terms of reading, for example, read a broad range of topics: the Quran, its explanation, the biography of the Prophet, peace and blessings be upon him and his Companions, hadith, Islamic jurisprudence, history, literature, books of general knowledge, and so forth.

Distribute your time between worship and enjoying what is lawful, from visiting friends, entertaining guests, playing sports, or going on excursions: you will find yourself to be a lively and bright person, because the soul delights in variety and things that are new.

Allah says: "Did We not expand for you, [O Muhammad], your breast?" (94:1)

أَلَمْ نَشْرَحْ لَكَ صَدْرَكَ ﴿١﴾

The message of this verse embraces all those who carry the truth, who see the light, and who tread the path of guidance. So is one whose breast Allah has expanded to [accept] Islam and he is upon a light from his Lord [like one whose heart rejects it]? Then woe to those whose hearts are hardened against the remembrance of Allah. Those are in manifest error. (39:22)

أَفَمَن شَرَحَ ٱللَّهُ صَدْرَهُ لِلْإِسْلَٰمِ فَهُوَ عَلَىٰ نُورٍ مِّن رَّبِّهِۦ فَوَيْلٌ لِّلْقَٰسِيَةِ قُلُوبُهُم مِّن ذِكْرِ ٱللَّهِ أُوْلَٰٓئِكَ فِى ضَلَٰلٍ مُّبِينٍ ﴿٢٢﴾

Therefore there is a truth that causes the heart to be opened and a falsehood that causes it to harden. And whosoever Allah wills to guide, He opens his breast to Islam)

So whoever Allah wants to guide - He expands his breast to [contain] Islam; and whoever He wants to misguide - He makes his breast tight and constricted as though he were climbing into the sky. Thus does Allah place defilement upon those who do not believe. (6:125)

فَمَن يُرِدِ ٱللَّهُ أَن يَهۡدِيَهُۥ يَشۡرَحۡ صَدۡرَهُۥ لِلۡإِسۡلَٰمِ وَمَن يُرِدۡ أَن يُضِلَّهُۥ يَجۡعَلۡ صَدۡرَهُۥ ضَيِّقًا حَرَجًا كَأَنَّمَا يَصَّعَّدُ فِي ٱلسَّمَآءِ كَذَٰلِكَ يَجۡعَلُ ٱللَّهُ ٱلرِّجۡسَ عَلَى ٱلَّذِينَ لَا يُؤۡمِنُونَ ﴿١٢٥﴾

So the acceptance of and adherence to this Religion is a goal that cannot be achieved except by the one who is blessed.

The Benefits of Marriage

A tear that runs down a believer's cheek is more beneficial than a thousand raindrops on the earth. The young child says: when I will become a bigger girl. The girl says: when I become a teenager, and when that time comes, she says: when I will marry. What about after marriage? And what comes after all of these stages? When a servant of Allāh marries, they perfect half their religion; and let them fear Allāh in the remaining half.

Marriage in Islam is something positive for those that have reached the age of maturity. It should not never be delayed if there is a good partner available and also the means to establish a family. Divorced people, widows, and widowers are encouraged to find someone and to re-marry. In Islam, religious celibacy is discouraged. Because it is very tough to control your physical desires even if you fast each day.

Although marriage is not a compulsory duty, nevertheless, Islam favors marriage. But do not marry polytheistic women until they believe. And a believing slave woman is better than a polytheist, even though she might please you. And do not marry polytheistic men [to your women] until they believe. And a believing slave is better than a polytheist, even though he might please you. Those invite [you] to the Fire, but Allāh invites to Paradise and to forgiveness, by His permission. And He makes clear His verses to the people that perhaps they may remember. (2:221)

وَلَا تَنكِحُوا۟ ٱلْمُشْرِكَٰتِ حَتَّىٰ يُؤْمِنَّ ۚ وَلَأَمَةٌ مُّؤْمِنَةٌ خَيْرٌ مِّن مُّشْرِكَةٍ وَلَوْ أَعْجَبَتْكُمْ ۗ وَلَا تُنكِحُوا۟ ٱلْمُشْرِكِينَ حَتَّىٰ يُؤْمِنُوا۟ ۚ وَلَعَبْدٌ مُّؤْمِنٌ خَيْرٌ مِّن مُّشْرِكٍ وَلَوْ أَعْجَبَكُمْ ۗ أُو۟لَٰٓئِكَ يَدْعُونَ إِلَى ٱلنَّارِ ۖ وَٱللَّهُ يَدْعُوٓا۟ إِلَى ٱلْجَنَّةِ وَٱلْمَغْفِرَةِ بِإِذْنِهِۦ ۖ وَيُبَيِّنُ ءَايَٰتِهِۦ لِلنَّاسِ لَعَلَّهُمْ يَتَذَكَّرُونَ ۝

Prohibited for marriage are your mothers, your daughters, your sisters, your father's sisters, your mother's sisters, your brother's daughters, your sister's daughters, your [milk] mothers who nursed you, your sisters through nursing, your wives' mothers, and your step-daughters under your guardianship [born] of your wives unto whom you have gone in. But if you have not gone in unto them, there is no sin upon you. And [also prohibited are] the wives of your sons who are from your [own] loins, and that you take in marriage two sisters simultaneously, except for what has already occurred. Indeed, Allāh is ever Forgiving and Merciful. (4:23)

حُرِّمَتْ عَلَيْكُمْ أُمَّهَٰتُكُمْ وَبَنَاتُكُمْ وَأَخَوَٰتُكُمْ وَعَمَّٰتُكُمْ وَخَٰلَٰتُكُمْ وَبَنَاتُ ٱلْأَخِ وَبَنَاتُ ٱلْأُخْتِ وَأُمَّهَٰتُكُمُ ٱلَّٰتِىٓ أَرْضَعْنَكُمْ وَأَخَوَٰتُكُم مِّنَ ٱلرَّضَٰعَةِ وَأُمَّهَٰتُ نِسَآئِكُمْ وَرَبَٰٓئِبُكُمُ ٱلَّٰتِى فِى حُجُورِكُم مِّن نِّسَآئِكُمُ ٱلَّٰتِى دَخَلْتُم بِهِنَّ فَإِن لَّمْ تَكُونُوا۟ دَخَلْتُم بِهِنَّ فَلَا جُنَاحَ عَلَيْكُمْ وَحَلَٰٓئِلُ أَبْنَآئِكُمُ ٱلَّذِينَ مِنْ أَصْلَٰبِكُمْ وَأَن تَجْمَعُوا۟ بَيْنَ ٱلْأُخْتَيْنِ إِلَّا مَا قَدْ سَلَفَ إِنَّ ٱللَّهَ كَانَ غَفُورًا رَّحِيمًا ﴿٢٣﴾

And remember that day, when the hypocrite men and hypocrite women will say to those who believed, "Wait for us that we may acquire some of your light." It will be said, "Go back behind you and seek light." And a wall will be placed between them with a door, its interior containing mercy, but on the outside of it is torment. (57:13)

يَوْمَ يَقُولُ ٱلْمُنَٰفِقُونَ وَٱلْمُنَٰفِقَٰتُ لِلَّذِينَ ءَامَنُوا ٱنظُرُونَا نَقْتَبِسْ مِن نُّورِكُمْ قِيلَ ٱرْجِعُوا وَرَآءَكُمْ فَٱلْتَمِسُوا نُورًا فَضُرِبَ بَيْنَهُم بِسُورٍ لَّهُۥ بَابٌ بَاطِنُهُۥ فِيهِ ٱلرَّحْمَةُ وَظَٰهِرُهُۥ مِن قِبَلِهِ ٱلْعَذَابُ ﴿١٣﴾

Marriage is a relationship between a <u>man</u> and a <u>woman</u> that provides for the lawful development and expression of love. It links personal care with physical love and responsibility towards the partner and towards the sons and daughters that may be born of the union.

It is truly only in the context of marriage that women are protected for their vital role as mothers of the next generation. Modern experiments with free sex and single-parent families have confirmed the disruptive social and economic effects, more on women and their tragic effects for the next generation. Children of single-parent families are often more lost. They need both parents for a secure and well-adjusted life.

The benefit of marriage is important not only to the sons and daughters and wife, but also to the man. Divorce causes suffering to the family, but also causes even more depression among men than women. Women provide psychological comfort as well as physical love and should not be under-estimated.

Men without comforts of a wife and family are much more exposed to temptations of unlawful sexual relations and deviant unlawful behavior.

It cannot be a mere coincidence that the decline of marriage in today's world has been accompanied by a rise in homosexuality, child abuse, murder, and rape - even of baby girls, boys, and old women. What is wrong with humanity? Have we forgotten the Quran or are we ignoring it? We will be questioned by Allāh how we used our time. So let us use it wisely.

Nothing is hidden from Allāh, on earth or in the heavens. In their hearts is disease, so Allah has increased their disease; and for them is a painful punishment because they [habitually] used to lie. (2:10)

فِى قُلُوبِهِم مَّرَضٌ فَزَادَهُمُ ٱللَّهُ مَرَضًا ۖ وَلَهُمْ عَذَابٌ أَلِيمٌۢ بِمَا كَانُوا۟ يَكْذِبُونَ ﴿١٠﴾

Allāh has referred to the marriage as one of Allāh's beautiful wonders. Marriage enshrines love, the greatest and most transforming of all human emotions. And of His signs is that He created for you from yourselves mates that you may find tranquility in them; and He placed between you affection and mercy.

Indeed in that are signs for a people who give thought. (30:21)

وَمِنْ ءَايَتِهِۦٓ أَنْ خَلَقَ لَكُم مِّنْ أَنفُسِكُمْ أَزْوَٰجًا لِّتَسْكُنُوٓا۟ إِلَيْهَا وَجَعَلَ بَيْنَكُم مَّوَدَّةً وَرَحْمَةً إِنَّ فِى ذَٰلِكَ لَءَايَٰتٍ لِّقَوْمٍ يَتَفَكَّرُونَ ۝

In another verse of the Qur'an Allāh says: It has been made permissible for you the night preceding fasting to go to your wives [for sexual relations ... Allah has decreed for you. And eat and drink until the white thread ... to you from the black thread [of night]. Then complete the fast until the sunset ... (2:187)

أُحِلَّ لَكُمْ لَيْلَةَ ٱلصِّيَامِ ٱلرَّفَثُ إِلَىٰ نِسَآئِكُمْ هُنَّ لِبَاسٌ لَّكُمْ وَأَنتُمْ لِبَاسٌ لَّهُنَّ عَلِمَ ٱللَّهُ أَنَّكُمْ كُنتُمْ تَخْتَانُونَ أَنفُسَكُمْ فَتَابَ عَلَيْكُمْ وَعَفَا عَنكُمْ فَٱلْـَٰٔنَ بَٰشِرُوهُنَّ وَٱبْتَغُوا۟ مَا كَتَبَ ٱللَّهُ لَكُمْ وَكُلُوا۟ وَٱشْرَبُوا۟ حَتَّىٰ يَتَبَيَّنَ لَكُمُ ٱلْخَيْطُ ٱلْأَبْيَضُ مِنَ ٱلْخَيْطِ ٱلْأَسْوَدِ مِنَ ٱلْفَجْرِ ثُمَّ أَتِمُّوا۟ ٱلصِّيَامَ إِلَى ٱلَّيْلِ وَلَا تُبَٰشِرُوهُنَّ وَأَنتُمْ عَٰكِفُونَ فِى ٱلْمَسَٰجِدِ تِلْكَ حُدُودُ ٱللَّهِ فَلَا تَقْرَبُوهَا كَذَٰلِكَ يُبَيِّنُ ٱللَّهُ ءَايَٰتِهِۦ لِلنَّاسِ لَعَلَّهُمْ يَتَّقُونَ ۝

Comfort, protection and intimacy are all contained in the marriage relationship as it is intended to be. The Prophet, peace and blessings be upon him, said that: "You have seen nothing like marriage for increasing the love of two people."

Marriage is not a prison but a beautiful step, a safe sanctuary, a source of contentment, tranquility, comfort, and spiritual gift through shared commitment and experience.

If marriage is turned into an arena for conflict, discontent, oppression, or abuse, then it is failing to fulfill its proper role. Therefore every effort must be made to make sure that there is strong compatibility between a woman and a man before they are betrothed. Also, every effort must be taken to avoid the souring of a marriage once it is created.

Every person is capable of obeying Allah in every way. Every person is capable of performing your daily tasks, no matter how difficult they are, and every person is capable of living happily. But when one actually reaches old age and looks back, he is scorched by a cold wind. He lost out on his whole life that dwindled away without ever living inside of it. And thus we learn, only when it is too late, that life is to be lived in every breathing minute and hour. Such is the state of those who put off repenting from their sins. One of our pious scholars once said: "I warn you of delaying and saying that I will do it later, for this is a phrase that prevents one from doing good and causes one to fall behind in deeds of righteousness."

Leave them eat and enjoy themselves and be diverted by [false] hope, for they are going to know. (15:3)

ذَرْهُمْ يَأْكُلُواْ وَيَتَمَتَّعُواْ وَيُلْهِهِمُ ٱلْأَمَلُ فَسَوْفَ يَعْلَمُونَ ﴿٣﴾

Or [they are] like darknesses within an unfathomable sea which is covered by waves, upon which are waves, over which are clouds - darknesses, some of them upon others. When one puts out his hand [therein], he can hardly see it. And he to whom Allah has not granted light - for him there is no light. (24:40)

أَوْ كَظُلُمَٰتٍ فِي بَحْرٍ لُّجِّيٍّ يَغْشَىٰهُ مَوْجٌ مِّن فَوْقِهِۦ مَوْجٌ مِّن فَوْقِهِۦ سَحَابٌ ۚ ظُلُمَٰتٌۢ بَعْضُهَا فَوْقَ بَعْضٍ إِذَآ أَخْرَجَ يَدَهُۥ لَمْ يَكَدْ يَرَىٰهَا ۗ وَمَن لَّمْ يَجْعَلِ ٱللَّهُ لَهُۥ نُورًا فَمَا لَهُۥ مِن نُّورٍ ۝

Indeed, We guided him to the way, be he grateful or be he ungrateful. (76:3)

إِنَّا هَدَيْنَٰهُ ٱلسَّبِيلَ إِمَّا شَاكِرًا وَإِمَّا كَفُورًا ۝

Always trust in Allah's plan. If it has been a bad day, consider that this day will not occur again. Better and more beautiful and complete is the hadith: "And pray as if this is your farewell and last prayer."

Always put it into your mind that today is your last day. So make a fresh repentance, do good deeds, and strive to be obedient to your Lord, the Almighty and His Messenger, peace and blessing be upon him.

Do not grieve and ask yourself the following questions

1. Do I put off living in the present because of fears and apprehensions about the future or because of hopes of the magical garden beyond the horizon?

2. Do I embitter my present life by mulling over events that occurred in the past?

3. Do I wake up in the morning with an intention of spending my day usefully?

4. Do I find that I am benefiting from my life when I try to concentrate on a present situation or task?

5. When will I begin to live in the present moment, without worrying too much about the past and future? Next week? Tomorrow? Or today?

The relationship between husband and wife is the most honorific relation in Islam. Your decision to marry is a spiritual covenant that is rooted in a commitment to one another that is completed through the love of Allah.

And of His signs is that He created for you from yourselves mates that you may find tranquility in them; and He placed between you affection and mercy. Indeed in that are signs for a people who give thought. (30:21)

وَمِنۡ ءَايَٰتِهِۦٓ أَنۡ خَلَقَ لَكُم مِّنۡ أَنفُسِكُمۡ أَزۡوَٰجًا لِّتَسۡكُنُوٓا۟ إِلَيۡهَا وَجَعَلَ بَيۡنَكُم مَّوَدَّةً وَرَحۡمَةً إِنَّ فِي ذَٰلِكَ لَأٓيَٰتٍ لِّقَوۡمٍ يَتَفَكَّرُونَ ﴿٢١﴾

Matrimonial services

FarouqMasjid@gmail.com

There are many matrimonial and matching services. Your local masjid might provide this service. The important thing is to do your research. Ask your friends and family if there is a service they would recommend. If you would Farouq Masjid to send you marriage proposals when possible, please send the following:

- Your full name and address
- Picture
- Gender
- Age
- Height
- Marital Status
- Children
- Your Ethnic Origin & Spouse Preference
- Education
- Profession
- Country and residency status
- Hijab
- Phone, Email, and mailing address
- Spouse Preferences and his/her age

Choosing the Right Partner

Marriages can go wrong quickly if the couple are not compatible. Therefore, prevention in this respect is better than cure. It is very important to ensure that one is looking for the right qualities in a partner. The Prophet (peace be upon him) said: "A woman may be married for four reasons:

1. Her Wealth
2. Her Rank
3. Her Beauty
4. Her Religious Character

Choose the woman with the _Religious Character_ and prosper."

The same applies in the choice of a man by a woman. It is very foolish for a woman to choose a man because of his looks, wealth, or of high social status if he lacks good religious character. The first three are never a guarantee of happiness.

A man of genuinely religious character is most likely to understand and to observe the Islamic requirement of kindness to his wife and children, and to abide by Allāh's laws with regard to his behavior towards everyone. His consciousness of Allāh (swt) acts as a very strong restraint on his behavior. Whatever are his weakness, at least he does not deliberately try to do wrong.

Men and women should pray regularly for a good partner. They should also try to find out as much as possible about the character of the person. The Prophet, peace be upon him, advised us that a couple thinking of marriage must be given the chance to meet each other (in the presence of a relative) in order to determine at least basic compatibility. And give the women [upon marriage] their [bridal] gifts graciously. But if they give up willingly to you anything of it, then take it in satisfaction and ease. (4:4)

وَءَاتُواْ ٱلنِّسَآءَ صَدُقَـٰتِهِنَّ نِحْلَةً فَإِن طِبْنَ لَكُمْ عَن شَىْءٍ مِّنْهُ نَفْسًا فَكُلُوهُ هَنِيٓـًٔا مَّرِيٓـًٔا ﴿٤﴾

And marry the unmarried among you and the righteous among your male slaves and female slaves. If they should be poor, Allah will enrich them from His bounty, and Allah is all-Encompassing and Knowing. (24:32)

وَأَنكِحُوا۟ ٱلْأَيَـٰمَىٰ مِنكُمْ وَٱلصَّـٰلِحِينَ مِنْ عِبَادِكُمْ وَإِمَآئِكُمْ إِن يَكُونُوا۟ فُقَرَآءَ يُغْنِهِمُ ٱللَّهُ مِن فَضْلِهِۦ ۗ وَٱللَّهُ وَٰسِعٌ عَلِيمٌ ﴿٣٢﴾

O Prophet, indeed We have made lawful to you your wives to whom you have given their due compensation and those your right hand possesses from what Allah has returned to you [of captives] and the daughters of your paternal uncles and the daughters of your paternal aunts and the daughters of your maternal uncles and the daughters of your maternal aunts who emigrated with you and a believing woman if she gives herself to the Prophet [and] if the Prophet wishes to marry her, [this is] only for you, excluding the [other] believers.

We certainly know what We have made obligatory upon them concerning their wives and those their right hands possess, [but this is for you] in order that there will be upon you no discomfort. And ever is Allah Forgiving and Merciful. (33:50)

يَٰٓأَيُّهَا ٱلنَّبِىُّ إِنَّآ أَحْلَلْنَا لَكَ أَزْوَٰجَكَ ٱلَّٰتِىٓ ءَاتَيْتَ أُجُورَهُنَّ وَمَا مَلَكَتْ يَمِينُكَ مِمَّآ أَفَآءَ ٱللَّهُ عَلَيْكَ وَبَنَاتِ عَمِّكَ وَبَنَاتِ عَمَّٰتِكَ وَبَنَاتِ خَالِكَ وَبَنَاتِ خَٰلَٰتِكَ ٱلَّٰتِى هَاجَرْنَ مَعَكَ وَٱمْرَأَةً مُّؤْمِنَةً إِن وَهَبَتْ نَفْسَهَا لِلنَّبِىِّ إِنْ أَرَادَ ٱلنَّبِىُّ أَن يَسْتَنكِحَهَا خَالِصَةً لَّكَ مِن دُونِ ٱلْمُؤْمِنِينَ قَدْ عَلِمْنَا مَا فَرَضْنَا عَلَيْهِمْ فِىٓ أَزْوَٰجِهِمْ وَمَا مَلَكَتْ أَيْمَٰنُهُمْ لِكَيْلَا يَكُونَ عَلَيْكَ حَرَجٌ وَكَانَ ٱللَّهُ غَفُورًا رَّحِيمًا ۝

O you who have believed, when the believing women come to you as emigrants, examine them. Allah is most knowing as to their faith. And if you know them to be believers, then do not return them to the disbelievers; they are not lawful [wives] for them, nor are they lawful [husbands] for them. But give the disbelievers what they have spent. And there is no blame upon you if you marry them when you have given them their due compensation. And hold not to marriage bonds with disbelieving women, but ask for what you have spent and let them ask for what they have spent. That is the judgment of Allah; He judges between you. And Allah is Knowing and Wise. (60:10)

يَٰٓأَيُّهَا ٱلَّذِينَ ءَامَنُوٓاْ إِذَا جَآءَكُمُ ٱلْمُؤْمِنَٰتُ مُهَٰجِرَٰتٍ فَٱمْتَحِنُوهُنَّ ٱللَّهُ أَعْلَمُ بِإِيمَٰنِهِنَّ فَإِنْ عَلِمْتُمُوهُنَّ مُؤْمِنَٰتٍ فَلَا تَرْجِعُوهُنَّ إِلَى ٱلْكُفَّارِ لَا هُنَّ حِلٌّ لَّهُمْ وَلَا هُمْ يَحِلُّونَ لَهُنَّ وَءَاتُوهُم مَّآ أَنفَقُواْ وَلَا جُنَاحَ عَلَيْكُمْ أَن تَنكِحُوهُنَّ إِذَآ ءَاتَيْتُمُوهُنَّ أُجُورَهُنَّ وَلَا تُمْسِكُواْ بِعِصَمِ ٱلْكَوَافِرِ وَسْـَٔلُواْ مَآ أَنفَقْتُمْ وَلْيَسْـَٔلُواْ مَآ أَنفَقُواْ ذَٰلِكُمْ حُكْمُ ٱللَّهِ يَحْكُمُ بَيْنَكُمْ وَٱللَّهُ عَلِيمٌ حَكِيمٌ ﴿١٠﴾

O Prophet, when the believing women come to you pledging to you that they will not associate anything with Allah, nor will they steal, nor will they commit unlawful sexual intercourse, nor will they kill their children, nor will they bring forth a slander they have invented between their arms and legs, nor will they disobey you in what is right - then accept their pledge and ask forgiveness for them of Allah. Indeed, Allah is Forgiving and Merciful. (60:12)

يَـٰٓأَيُّهَا ٱلنَّبِىُّ إِذَا جَآءَكَ ٱلْمُؤْمِنَـٰتُ يُبَايِعْنَكَ عَلَىٰٓ أَن لَّا يُشْرِكْنَ بِٱللَّهِ شَيْـًٔا وَلَا يَسْرِقْنَ وَلَا يَزْنِينَ وَلَا يَقْتُلْنَ أَوْلَـٰدَهُنَّ وَلَا يَأْتِينَ بِبُهْتَـٰنٍ يَفْتَرِينَهُۥ بَيْنَ أَيْدِيهِنَّ وَأَرْجُلِهِنَّ وَلَا يَعْصِينَكَ فِى مَعْرُوفٍ فَبَايِعْهُنَّ وَٱسْتَغْفِرْ لَهُنَّ ٱللَّهَ إِنَّ ٱللَّهَ غَفُورٌ رَّحِيمٌ ۝

Allah presents an example of those who disbelieved: the wife of Noah and the wife of Lot. They were under two of Our righteous servants but betrayed them, so those prophets did not avail them from Allah at all, and it was said: "Enter the Fire with those who enter."

ضَرَبَ ٱللَّهُ مَثَلًا لِّلَّذِينَ كَفَرُوا۟ ٱمْرَأَتَ نُوحٍ وَٱمْرَأَتَ لُوطٍ كَانَتَا تَحْتَ عَبْدَيْنِ مِنْ عِبَادِنَا صَـٰلِحَيْنِ فَخَانَتَاهُمَا فَلَمْ يُغْنِيَا عَنْهُمَا مِنَ ٱللَّهِ شَيْـًٔا وَقِيلَ ٱدْخُلَا ٱلنَّارَ مَعَ ٱلدَّـٰخِلِينَ ۝

And Allah presents an example of those who believed: the wife of Pharaoh, when she said, "My Lord, build for me near You a house in Paradise and save me from Pharaoh and his deeds and save me from the wrongdoing people." (66:11)

وَضَرَبَ ٱللَّهُ مَثَلًا لِّلَّذِينَ ءَامَنُوا۟ ٱمْرَأَتَ فِرْعَوْنَ إِذْ قَالَتْ رَبِّ ٱبْنِ لِى عِندَكَ بَيْتًا فِى ٱلْجَنَّةِ وَنَجِّنِى مِن فِرْعَوْنَ وَعَمَلِهِۦ وَنَجِّنِى مِنَ ٱلْقَوْمِ ٱلظَّـٰلِمِينَ ﴿١١﴾

Prophet Muhammad, peace be upon him said: "Many men reached perfection but none among the women reached perfection except Mary (Mariam), the daughter of Imran, and Asya, Pharaoh's wife. And the superiority of Aisha to other women is like the superiority of Tharid to other kinds of food." (Al-Bukhari)

The Death of a Child

She said: "Woe to me! Shall I give birth while I am an old woman and this, my husband, is an old man? Indeed, this is an amazing thing!" (11:72)

قَالَتْ يَٰوَيْلَتَىٰٓ ءَأَلِدُ وَأَنَا۠ عَجُوزٌ وَهَٰذَا بَعْلِى شَيْخًا إِنَّ هَٰذَالَشَىْءٌ عَجِيبٌ ۝

And [recall] when We saved your forefathers from the people of Pharaoh, who afflicted you with the worst torment, slaughtering your [newborn] sons and keeping your females alive. And in that was a great trial from your Lord. (2:49)

وَإِذْ نَجَّيْنَٰكُم مِّنْ ءَالِ فِرْعَوْنَ يَسُومُونَكُمْ سُوٓءَ ٱلْعَذَابِ يُذَبِّحُونَ أَبْنَآءَكُمْ وَيَسْتَحْيُونَ نِسَآءَكُمْ وَفِى ذَٰلِكُم بَلَآءٌ مِّن رَّبِّكُمْ عَظِيمٌ ۝

When Allah, the Merciful and Exalted, takes something away from you, He compensates you with something better, but only if you are patient and seek your reward from Him. The Prophet, peace and blessings be upon him said:

"Whoever has his eyesight taken away from him and is then patient, he will be compensated for it with Paradise."

In Surat Al-Kahf aya 74, the journey between Al-Khidr and Moses, Al-Khidr kills an innocent boy and later on explains to Moses that the boy's parents were of the believers and they feared lest he (the boy) should oppress them with rebellion and disbelief. Al-Khidr said: "This is the parting between me and you. I will tell you the interpretation of (those) things over which you were unable to hold patience. (18:78)

قَالَ هَٰذَا فِرَاقُ بَيۡنِي وَبَيۡنِكَ سَأُنَبِّئُكَ بِتَأۡوِيلِ مَا لَمۡ تَسۡتَطِع عَّلَيۡهِ صَبۡرًا ﴿٧٨﴾

As for the ship, it belonged to poor people working in the sea. So I wished to make a defective damage in it, as there was a king after them who seized every ship by force. And as for the boy, his parents were believers, and we feared lest he should oppress them by rebellion and disbelief.

So we intended that their Lord should change him for them for one better in righteousness and near to mercy. And as for the wall, it belonged to two orphan boys in the town; and there was under it a treasure belonging to them, and their father was a righteous man, and your Lord intended that they should attain their age of full strength and take out their treasure as a mercy from your Lord. And I did it not of my own accord. That is the interpretation of those (things) over which you could not hold patience. (Surah 18: 60-82)

Allah the Generous, in His infinite mercy, gave the boy's parents a beautiful girl. That girl became the mother of Prophet Jonah (Yunus), peace be upon him.

The Prophet, peace be upon him, said in another hadith: "Whoever loses a loved one from the people of this world and then seeks his recompense with his Lord, will be compensated with Paradise."

So do not feel excessive sorrow over some misfortune, because the One Who decreed it has with Him Paradise: recompense and a great reward.

Those that are afflicted in this world and are close to Allah will be praised in the highest part of heaven: "Peace be upon you for what you patiently endured. And excellent is the final home." (13:24)

سَلَـٰمٌ عَلَيْكُم بِمَا صَبَرْتُمْ فَنِعْمَ عُقْبَى ٱلدَّارِ ﴿٢٤﴾

We must contemplate the reward one receives for forbearing hardship.

Those are the ones upon whom are blessings from their Lord and mercy. And it is those who are the [rightly] guided. (2:157)

أُوْلَٰٓئِكَ عَلَيْهِمْ صَلَوَٰتٌ مِّن رَّبِّهِمْ وَرَحْمَةٌ ۖ وَأُوْلَٰٓئِكَ هُمُ ٱلْمُهْتَدُونَ ﴿١٥٧﴾

Truly, the life of this world is very short and its treasures are few. The Hereafter is better and everlasting, and whosoever is afflicted here shall find his reward there. And whosoever works hard here shall find ease there. As for those who cling to this world, who are attached to it, and who are in love with it, the hardest thing for them to bear would be to lose the world's comforts and riches: they desire to enjoy this life alone. Because of this desire, they do not react to misfortune as well as others do.

What they perceive around them is this life alone: they are blind to its impermanence and insignificance. If you are patient you lose nothing; and though you may not perceive it, you are profiting. The person who is afflicted with hardship should reflect upon the outcome in the Hereafter, the outcome for those who are patient.

On the [same] Day the hypocrite men and hypocrite women will say to those who believed: "Wait for us that we may acquire some of your light." It will be said: "Go back behind you and seek light." And a wall will be placed between them with a door, its interior containing mercy, but on the outside of it is torment. (57:13)

يَوْمَ يَقُولُ ٱلْمُنَٰفِقُونَ وَٱلْمُنَٰفِقَٰتُ لِلَّذِينَ ءَامَنُوا ٱنظُرُونَا نَقْتَبِسْ مِن نُّورِكُمْ قِيلَ ٱرْجِعُوا وَرَآءَكُمْ فَٱلْتَمِسُوا نُورًا فَضُرِبَ بَيْنَهُم بِسُورٍ لَّهُۥ بَابٌۢ بَاطِنُهُۥ فِيهِ ٱلرَّحْمَةُ وَظَٰهِرُهُۥ مِن قِبَلِهِ ٱلْعَذَابُ ﴿١٣﴾

Sincerity and Trust

The Prophet (peace and blessing be upon him) said: "Religion is sincerity." A man asked: "Sincerity to whom?" Peace be upon him replied: "To Allāh, His Book, His Prophets, and His Last Messenger."

Therefore, sincerity is strongly identified with true religious belief. Sincerity towards his wife, her husband, is an essential requirement for a husband and a wife. Firstly it implies having each other's interests at heart and wanting only good for each other. Secondly it implies truthfulness so that they learn to trust each other in word and deed. They would never tell each other a lie even in small matters because this will sow the seeds of doubt about trustworthiness in greater matters.

Once trust is gone, it is hard to rebuild it. If you tell a lie to cover up something else you did, this only compounds the offence. You should in all circumstances repent very sincerely to Allāh (swt) and seek His forgiveness. You should then tell the truth and seek forgiveness unless the sin is a matter that could destroy the marriage. In such a case, you must repent to Allāh silently and amend the behavior in future.

The Messenger of Allāh, peace and blessings be upon him, directed people to forgive those who ask for forgiveness. The person who sincerely repents, tells the truth and seeks forgiveness may be able to re-establish trust. However, the shameless liar leaves the partner in a state of constant stress, doubt, and unworthy of trust. You must never throw away that basic trust for anything.

Another aspect of sincerity is supporting each other in doing what is lawful and avoiding what is wrong doing. Allāh says: The believing men and believing women are allies of one another.

They enjoin what is right and forbid what is wrong and establish prayer and give zakah and obey Allāh and His Messenger. Those - Allāh will have mercy upon them. Indeed, Allāh is Exalted in Might and Wise. (9:71)

وَٱلْمُؤْمِنُونَ وَٱلْمُؤْمِنَٰتُ بَعْضُهُمْ أَوْلِيَآءُ بَعْضٍ يَأْمُرُونَ بِٱلْمَعْرُوفِ وَيَنْهَوْنَ عَنِ ٱلْمُنكَرِ وَيُقِيمُونَ ٱلصَّلَوٰةَ وَيُؤْتُونَ ٱلزَّكَوٰةَ وَيُطِيعُونَ ٱللَّهَ وَرَسُولَهُۥٓ أُوْلَٰٓئِكَ سَيَرْحَمُهُمُ ٱللَّهُ إِنَّ ٱللَّهَ عَزِيزٌ حَكِيمٌ ﴿٧١﴾

This view on the acceptability of silence is based on comparison with a Hadith which allows for the use of a small "white lie." For example, someone that tried to reunite two people that were estranged: "The person is not a liar when reconciling two people, and speaks good, and adds good from himself." (Hadith from Bukhari, Muslim, Tirmidhi, and Abu Dawud)

Heed unto Allāh and His Messenger, peace and blessings be upon him. It is they upon whom Allāh will bestow His mercy and grace: Indeed, Allāh is the Merciful and Most Wise.

Both the husband and wife should be obedient and faithful to Allāh and must help all the family to live a righteous life. There must always be mutual counselling within the family. The Messenger of Allāh, peace and blessing be upon him, long after the death his first wife, Khadijah, the Prophet always praised Khadijah for her loyalty and moral support during their married life together.

The husband and wife must trust each other. O you who believe! Avoid much suspicions, indeed some suspicions are sins. And spy not, neither backbite one another. Would one of you like to eat the flesh of his dead brother? You would hate it (so hate backbiting). And fear Allah. Verily, Allah is the One Who accepts repentance, Most Merciful. (49:12)

يَٰٓأَيُّهَا ٱلَّذِينَ ءَامَنُوا ٱجۡتَنِبُوا كَثِيرًا مِّنَ ٱلظَّنِّ إِنَّ بَعۡضَ ٱلظَّنِّ إِثۡمٌ وَلَا تَجَسَّسُوا وَلَا يَغۡتَب بَّعۡضُكُم بَعۡضًا أَيُحِبُّ أَحَدُكُمۡ أَن يَأۡكُلَ لَحۡمَ أَخِيهِ مَيۡتًا فَكَرِهۡتُمُوهُ وَٱتَّقُوا ٱللَّهَ إِنَّ ٱللَّهَ تَوَّابٌ رَّحِيمٌ ﴿١٢﴾

Negative assumptions are damaging. For example, if a husband senses that his wife is spying on him, he will lose the sense of security in his own home and could start to lock up his personal papers and effects. This may increase the wife's suspicions.

According to a Hadith the Prophet, peace and blessings be upon him, said that reading someone else's letters without permission is a sin. Wives may drive their husbands away by their snooping and spying. This will also be very distressing for the children to realize that the parents do not trust each other.

The Fundamentals of Trust

A wise person who was afflicted by misfortune. His brothers and sisters went to him and tried to console him over his loss. He answered: "I have put together a remedy that is composed of six ingredients." They asked him what those ingredients were, and he answered them and said:

1. Have a firm trust in Allah, the Almighty.
2. Resigning oneself to the clear fact that everything that is decreed by Allah will happen and will follow its unalterable course.
3. Patience has no substitute for the positive effect it has on the afflicted.
4. An unwavering belief in the implications of this phrase: "Without showing forbearance, what will I accomplish?"
5. Ask yourself: "why should I be a willful party to my own destruction?"
6. Knowing that from one hour to the next, circumstances are transformed and difficulties vanish."

Do not grieve if others inflict upon you pain or harm, and do not grieve if you are oppressed and hated. Ibn Taymiyah said: The believer does not seek quarrel or revenge; nor does he find blame or fault in others. Do not despair if your life is filled with obstacles or problems; rather, forbear and be patient. Patience, as opposed to anxiety, bears the fruit of comfort; and the one who does not voluntarily show patience will have it forced upon him by circumstances. Time showers everyone with misery until the arrows on the heart forms a strong cover. Then when the heart is struck again with another arrow, the blade of it strikes into the shaft of another, then you will live without a care for troubles. So do not be feel bad if someone refuses you a favor, or if you are frowned upon, or if the miserly person refuses to help. If by refraining from asking others, you prevent the sweat of humiliation from pouring down your face, then a wooden hut or a tent of cloth is better for you than a spacious house and a beautiful garden, material things that will only bring you worry and disquiet.

Tribulation is similar to sickness: it must always run its course before it goes away, and the one who is hasty in attempting to remove it often causes it to strengthen and to increase. It is important that the one who is afflicted by pain to be patient. He must wait with hope for relief, and he must be persistent in his prayers. So verily, with the hardship, there is relief. (94:5)

فَإِنَّ مَعَ ٱلْعُسْرِ يُسْرًا ۝

Verily, there is one hardship with two reliefs, so one hardship cannot overcome two reliefs. (94:6)

إِنَّ مَعَ ٱلْعُسْرِ يُسْرًا ۝

When My servants ask you, [O Muhammad], concerning Me - indeed I am near. I respond to the invocation of the supplicant when he calls upon Me. So let them respond to Me [by obedience] and believe in Me that they may be [rightly] guided. (2:186)

وَإِذَا سَأَلَكَ عِبَادِى عَنِّى فَإِنِّى قَرِيبٌ أُجِيبُ دَعْوَةَ ٱلدَّاعِ إِذَا دَعَانِ فَلْيَسْتَجِيبُوا۟ لِى وَلْيُؤْمِنُوا۟ بِى لَعَلَّهُمْ يَرْشُدُونَ ۝

The believers are only those who, when Allah is mentioned, feel a fear in their hearts and when His Verses (this Quran) are recited unto them, they (i.e. the Verses) increase their Faith; and they put their **trust** in their Lord (Alone); (8:2)

إِنَّمَا ٱلۡمُؤۡمِنُونَ ٱلَّذِينَ إِذَا ذُكِرَ ٱللَّهُ وَجِلَتۡ قُلُوبُهُمۡ وَإِذَا تُلِيَتۡ عَلَيۡهِمۡ ءَايَٰتُهُۥ زَادَتۡهُمۡ إِيمَٰنٗا وَعَلَىٰ رَبِّهِمۡ يَتَوَكَّلُونَ ﴿٢﴾

Say: "Nothing shall ever happen to us except what Allah has ordained for us. He is our Maula (Lord, Helper and Protector)." And in Allah let the believers put their trust. (9:51)

قُل لَّن يُصِيبَنَآ إِلَّا مَا كَتَبَ ٱللَّهُ لَنَا هُوَ مَوۡلَىٰنَا وَعَلَى ٱللَّهِ فَلۡيَتَوَكَّلِ ٱلۡمُؤۡمِنُونَ ﴿٥١﴾

I put my trust in Allah, my Lord and your Lord! There is not a moving (living) creature but He has grasp of its forelock. Verily, my Lord is on the Straight Path (the truth). (11:56)

إِنِّي تَوَكَّلْتُ عَلَى اللَّهِ رَبِّي وَرَبِّكُم مَّا مِن دَآبَّةٍ إِلَّا هُوَ ءَاخِذُۢ بِنَاصِيَتِهَآ إِنَّ رَبِّي عَلَىٰ صِرَٰطٍ مُّسْتَقِيمٍ ﴿٥٦﴾

And put your trust in the All-Mighty, the Most Merciful. (26:217)

وَتَوَكَّلْ عَلَى الْعَزِيزِ الرَّحِيمِ ﴿٢١٧﴾

Understanding your Husband

Most married couples only after marriage they become fully aware of each other's character, behaviors, tempers, likes and dislikes. There is always some period of adjustment after marriage. If all goes well, the honeymoon relationship grows into another dimension, a more mature love that is based on friendship, understanding of each other, but provided the partners do not behave so badly that they might kill the love altogether. To cultivate this permanent and lasting kind of love, a wife must try to study her husband so as to know how to make him happy. In addition to knowing his likes and dislikes, a wife should also try to sense his moods and to respond to them, and to anticipate his desires. It is this responsiveness based on understanding and sympathy that creates strong bonds between the wife and the husband.

The Messenger of Allāh, peace be upon him, said: "The world is a provision, and the finest provision of the world is to have a righteous wife." Peace be upon him also said: "Should I not tell you of the best treasure of man? It is a righteous wife: when she is near, she delights him; and when he tells her something, she is compliant; and when he is away from her, she looks after his interest."

In other words both have learned to respond to the needs of each other. And he loves her not by her physical beauty (which may fade) but by her loving actions and warmth. When he asks her to do something or not to do, she obeys with good will. She attends to his well-being and never hurts his feelings.

The husband is also comforted by the knowledge that his wife's concern for his well-being and welfare is not just a show but sincere. And she takes care of his business and interest when he is away. She also guards her chastity and honor when he is absent.

All these are the characteristics of an ideal Muslim wife and woman. She has good manners and moral integrity.

There is another Hadith by the Prophet of Allāh, peace be upon him that describes the opposite behavior and its effects. For example, a woman that talks harshly and her husband becomes upset because of her rudeness. She gains the anger of Allāh (swt) until she repents and tries to please her husband.

A woman that wants her marriage to last happily into old age must therefore learn these lessons. Lover will never last forever if a woman is harsh, rude and disagreeable. Allāh, the Almighty and Merciful, gives us a prayer in the Quran: And those who say, "Our Lord, grant us from among our wives and offspring comfort to our eyes and make us an example for the righteous." (25:74)

وَالَّذِينَ يَقُولُونَ رَبَّنَا هَبْ لَنَا مِنْ أَزْوَاجِنَا وَذُرِّيَّاتِنَا قُرَّةَ أَعْيُنٍ وَاجْعَلْنَا لِلْمُتَّقِينَ إِمَامًا ﴿٧٤﴾

Isolation from bad influences and distractions has positive effects. If applied with a correct understanding, isolation from people with bad characteristics can be most beneficial.

Ibn Taymiyah said: "At times, it is good for the worshipper to be isolated from others in order to pray, remember Allah, recite the Quran, and evaluate himself and his deeds. Also, isolation allows one to supplicate, seek forgiveness, stay away from evil, and so on."

Isolation from bad influences brings repose, honor, and dignity. It helps one to stay away from evil, it protects one's honor, and it saves time. It keeps one away from the jealous minded and those who take pleasure in your affliction. It promotes the remembrance of the Hereafter, and it allows one to reflect on the meeting with Allah.

In times of seclusion, one's thoughts may roam in that which is good and beneficial, in that which contains wisdom. Only Allah knows the full benefits of seclusion, for in seclusion, one's mind develops, views are ripened, the heart finds repose, and one finds himself to be in an ideal atmosphere for worship. By remaining isolated at times, one distances himself from trials, from flattering the person who deserves no praise, and from the eyes of jealous and envious persons. One is saved from the haughtiness of the proud and the follies of the idiot. In isolation, one's fault s, deeds, and sayings are all secluded behind a veil.

During periods of isolation, one is able to delve deep into a sea of ideas and concepts. In such a state, the mind is free to form its opinions. Isolated from the company of others, the soul is free to achieve a state of rapture and to hunt for the stimulating thought.

Many of the People of the Scripture wish they could turn you back to disbelief after you have believed, out of envy from themselves [even] after the truth has become clear to them. So pardon and overlook until Allah delivers His command. Indeed, Allah is over all things competent. (2:109)

وَدَّ كَثِيرٌ مِّنْ أَهْلِ ٱلْكِتَٰبِ لَوْ يَرُدُّونَكُم مِّنۢ بَعْدِ إِيمَٰنِكُمْ كُفَّارًا حَسَدًا مِّنْ عِندِ أَنفُسِهِم مِّنۢ بَعْدِ مَا تَبَيَّنَ لَهُمُ ٱلْحَقُّ ۖ فَٱعْفُواْ وَٱصْفَحُواْ حَتَّىٰ يَأْتِىَ ٱللَّهُ بِأَمْرِهِ ۗ إِنَّ ٱللَّهَ عَلَىٰ كُلِّ شَىْءٍ قَدِيرٌ ﴿١٠٩﴾

And do not wish for that by which Allah has made some of you exceed others. For men is a share of what they have earned, and for women is a share of what they have earned. And ask Allah of his bounty. Indeed Allah is ever, of all things, Knowing. (4:32)

وَلَا تَتَمَنَّوْاْ مَا فَضَّلَ ٱللَّهُ بِهِۦ بَعْضَكُمْ عَلَىٰ بَعْضٍ ۚ لِّلرِّجَالِ نَصِيبٌ مِّمَّا ٱكْتَسَبُواْ ۖ وَلِلنِّسَاءِ نَصِيبٌ مِّمَّا ٱكْتَسَبْنَ ۚ وَسْـَٔلُواْ ٱللَّهَ مِن فَضْلِهِۦٓ ۗ إِنَّ ٱللَّهَ كَانَ بِكُلِّ شَىْءٍ عَلِيمًا ﴿٣٢﴾

Authority and Obedience

In every human group there is always a leader, a hierarchy of authority so that the members work together for the common good. The head of every family should be the oldest man, the husband, by virtue of his role as the protector of the family. Allāh, the Most Merciful and the Mighty said: "Men are in charge of women by [right of] what Allāh has given one over the other and what they spend [for maintenance] from their wealth. So righteous women are devoutly obedient, guarding in [the husband's] absence what Allāh would have them guard. But those [wives] from whom you fear arrogance - [first] advise them; [then if they persist], forsake them in bed; and [finally], strike them. But if they obey you [once more], seek no means against them. Indeed, Allāh is ever Exalted and Grand." (4:34)

الرِّجَالُ قَوَّمُونَ عَلَى النِّسَآءِ بِمَا فَضَّلَ اللَّهُ بَعْضَهُمْ عَلَى بَعْضٍ
وَبِمَآ أَنفَقُوا مِنْ أَمْوَٰلِهِمْ فَالصَّلِحَتُ قَنِتَتُ
حَفِظَتُ لِلْغَيْبِ بِمَا حَفِظَ اللَّهُ وَالَّتِي تَخَافُونَ نُشُوزَهُنَّ
فَعِظُوهُنَّ وَاهْجُرُوهُنَّ فِي الْمَضَاجِعِ وَاضْرِبُوهُنَّ فَإِنْ
أَطَعْنَكُمْ فَلَا تَبْغُوا عَلَيْهِنَّ سَبِيلًا إِنَّ اللَّهَ كَانَ عَلِيًّا
كَبِيرًا ﴿٣٤﴾

Divorced women remain in waiting for three periods, and it is not lawful for them to conceal what Allāh has created in their wombs if they believe in Allāh and the Last Day. And their husbands have more right to take them back in this [period] if they want reconciliation. And due to the wives is similar to what is expected of them, according to what is reasonable. But the men have a degree over them [in responsibility and authority]. And Allāh is Exalted in Might and Wise. (2:228)

وَٱلْمُطَلَّقَٰتُ يَتَرَبَّصْنَ بِأَنفُسِهِنَّ ثَلَٰثَةَ قُرُوٓءٍ وَلَا يَحِلُّ لَهُنَّ أَن

يَكْتُمْنَ مَا خَلَقَ ٱللَّهُ فِىٓ أَرْحَامِهِنَّ إِن كُنَّ يُؤْمِنَّ بِٱللَّهِ وَٱلْيَوْمِ ٱلْءَاخِرِ ۚ

وَبُعُولَتُهُنَّ أَحَقُّ بِرَدِّهِنَّ فِى ذَٰلِكَ إِنْ أَرَادُوٓا۟ إِصْلَٰحًا ۚ وَلَهُنَّ مِثْلُ ٱلَّذِى عَلَيْهِنَّ

بِٱلْمَعْرُوفِ ۚ وَلِلرِّجَالِ عَلَيْهِنَّ دَرَجَةٌ ۗ وَٱللَّهُ عَزِيزٌ حَكِيمٌ ﴿٢٢٨﴾

This "level" of difference in legal rights in divorce and marriage is just a reflection of the husband's leadership role, and this in no way says that the woman is inferior. This point is stated by Allāh, the Almighty and the Merciful: "Never will I allow to be lost the work of [any] worker among you, whether male or female; you are of one another. So those who emigrated or were evicted from their homes or were harmed in My cause or fought or were killed - I will surely remove from them their misdeeds, and I will surely admit them to gardens beneath which rivers flow as reward from Allāh , and Allāh has with Him the best reward." (3:195)

فَٱسۡتَجَابَ لَهُمۡ رَبُّهُمۡ أَنِّي لَآ أُضِيعُ عَمَلَ عَٰمِلٍ مِّنكُم مِّن ذَكَرٍ أَوۡ أُنثَىٰ بَعۡضُكُم مِّنۢ بَعۡضٍ فَٱلَّذِينَ هَاجَرُواْ وَأُخۡرِجُواْ مِن دِيَٰرِهِمۡ وَأُوذُواْ فِي سَبِيلِي وَقَٰتَلُواْ وَقُتِلُواْ لَأُكَفِّرَنَّ عَنۡهُمۡ سَيِّئَاتِهِمۡ وَلَأُدۡخِلَنَّهُمۡ جَنَّٰتٍ تَجۡرِي مِن تَحۡتِهَا ٱلۡأَنۡهَٰرُ ثَوَابًا مِّنۡ عِندِ ٱللَّهِ ۚ وَٱللَّهُ عِندَهُۥ حُسۡنُ ٱلثَّوَابِ ﴿١٩٥﴾

The Messenger of Allāh (peace be upon him) is also said: "All people (men and women) are equal, as equal as the teeth of a comb. And there is no claim of merit of a white person over a black person, or an Arab over a non-Arab, or a male over a female. Only God-fearing people merit a preference with Allāh." All people are born equal, in the sense that no one brings any possession with him; and they die equal in the sense that they take back nothing of their worldly belongings. Allāh judges every person on the basis of his own merits and according to his own deeds.

A woman should therefore acknowledge her husband's administrative leadership and should never dispute it, and must never set herself up as a rival in taking ultimate decisions that affect the family, even if she is the breadwinner, providing the largest portion to household income. A ship with two captains quarreling sinks, and the ship will never reach home. Still, leadership in Islam also has duties. The leader must always be motivated by love and concern for those people under his care, who will certainly respond by loving their leader.

The Messenger of Allāh (peace be upon him) said: "The best of your leaders are those for whom you pray and who pray for you, and for whom you love and who love you, and the worst of your leaders are those whom you hate, and who hate you, and whom you curse and who curse you." All forms of tyranny, cruelty, oppression and exploitation of the poor and weak are condemned, and tyrants are warned. Allah may delay the penalty of oppression but He will never ignore it.

"You should fear the prayer of the oppressed, wronged, and persecuted, for truly there is no veil between them and Allāh (swt). Tyrants shall never enter into Paradise."

The leader must consult his followers always. See the chapter in the Quran that is called "Shura", meaning consultation. "And those who have responded to their lord and established prayer and whose affair is [determined by] consultation among themselves, and from what We have provided them, they spend." (42:38)

وَٱلَّذِينَ ٱسْتَجَابُوا۟ لِرَبِّهِمْ وَأَقَامُوا۟ ٱلصَّلَوٰةَ وَأَمْرُهُمْ شُورَىٰ بَيْنَهُمْ وَمِمَّا رَزَقْنَٰهُمْ يُنفِقُونَ ﴿٣٨﴾

Leadership in Islam is recognized as a responsibility. It exists at several levels both in public issues and in the family. The Messenger of Allāh (peace be upon him) said:

"Take care: everyone is a shepherd and each shall be asked concerning his flock. A leader is shepherd over his people, and he shall be asked concerning his flock. A man is a shepherd over everyone in his own house, and this man shall be asked concerning his flock. A woman is also a shepherd over her house and she shall be asked concerning her flock (husband, sons, and daughters). The servant is a shepherd over the property of his master, and the servant shall be asked about it. Each of you is a shepherd and each of you shall be asked about your own flock."

As can be read from this Hadith, the wife has a big role and responsibility within the family, running the household and raising the children. We shall return to this aspect of the wife's role in another section. In this section, we want to discuss the aspects of leadership and authority in the home. We want to also explain the use of the words "obeying" and "ordering" that are used in translating some Quranic verses.

The Arabic word "amr" has the meaning of "to ordain" or "to order". However, in the context of family life, "amr" clearly does not have the same meaning as in the army. The wife and the family are not a military unit, and for a man to shout out orders to his wife like a drill sergeant, would not be best, and definitely counter-productive.

The relationship of husband and wife is quite different. A healthy relationship is where the husband or wife does not need to hide or lie about money or property. If you cannot trust your life partner, then why marry them? A healthy relationship is where both husband and wife bring up their children equally. A husband and are described in the Quran but as "garments to each other," loving, sympathetic and protecting each other.

A study of the word "amr" in the Quran shows that it has many meanings, such as "biding," "commanding," "instructing" and "urging." For example in the Quran (2:168-9), Allāh said: "O mankind, eat from whatever is on earth [that is] lawful and good and do not follow the footsteps of Satan. Indeed, he is to you a clear enemy. He gives you 'amr' only to do evil, and to commit deeds of abomination, and to attribute to Allāh something of which you have no knowledge."

يَـٰٓأَيُّهَا ٱلنَّاسُ كُلُواْ مِمَّا فِى ٱلۡأَرۡضِ حَلَـٰلًا طَيِّبًا وَلَا تَتَّبِعُواْ خُطُوَٰتِ ٱلشَّيۡطَـٰنِۚ إِنَّهُۥ لَكُمۡ عَدُوٌّ مُّبِينٌ ﴿١٦٨﴾

He only orders you to evil and immorality and to say about Allāh what you do not know.

إِنَّمَا يَأۡمُرُكُم بِٱلسُّوٓءِ وَٱلۡفَحۡشَآءِ وَأَن تَقُولُواْ عَلَى ٱللَّهِ مَا لَا تَعۡلَمُونَ ﴿١٦٩﴾

How does Shaitan give 'amr' to people to do evil? Not by issuing commands but he whispers evil into the breasts of mankind. (114:5).

$$\text{ٱلَّذِى يُوَسْوِسُ فِى صُدُورِ ٱلنَّاسِ ۝}$$

Moreover, Allāh that the Shaitan has no power over His creatures unless they choose to follow him. "My servants - no authority will you have over them, except those who follow you of the deviators." (15:42)

$$\text{إِنَّ عِبَادِى لَيْسَ لَكَ عَلَيْهِمْ سُلْطَـٰنٌ إِلَّا مَنِ ٱتَّبَعَكَ مِنَ}$$
$$\text{ٱلْغَاوِينَ ۝}$$

And Satan will say when the matter has been concluded, "Indeed, Allah had promised you the promise of truth. And I promised you, but I betrayed you. But I had no authority over you except that I invited you, and you responded to me. So do not blame me; but blame yourselves. I cannot be called to your aid, nor can you be called to my aid. Indeed, I deny your association of me [with Allah] before. Indeed, for the wrongdoers is a painful punishment. (14:22)

وَقَالَ ٱلشَّيْطَٰنُ لَمَّا قُضِيَ ٱلْأَمْرُ إِنَّ ٱللَّهَ وَعَدَكُمْ وَعْدَ ٱلْحَقِّ وَوَعَدتُّكُمْ فَأَخْلَفْتُكُمْ وَمَا كَانَ لِيَ عَلَيْكُم مِّن سُلْطَٰنٍ إِلَّآ أَن دَعَوْتُكُمْ فَٱسْتَجَبْتُمْ لِي فَلَا تَلُومُونِي وَلُومُوٓا۟ أَنفُسَكُم مَّآ أَنَا۠ بِمُصْرِخِكُمْ وَمَآ أَنتُم بِمُصْرِخِيَّ إِنِّي كَفَرْتُ بِمَآ أَشْرَكْتُمُونِ مِن قَبْلُ إِنَّ ٱلظَّٰلِمِينَ لَهُمْ عَذَابٌ أَلِيمٌ ﴿٢٢﴾

And so, it is clear that 'amr' does mean "to order" or "to command" in all contexts. The word 'amr' then requires analysis and clarification according to its context. Then in the context of marriage, it may be understood to mean that the husband has authority as a leader in accordance with Islamic law. The husband with gentleness should tell his wife what he wants to be done to enlist her assistance. Everyone with an understanding of relationships will realize that this manner of communicating has a positive effect and is much more effective than screaming out orders in an arbitrary uncaring and inconsiderate approach.

Therefore, when asked to do something in a considerate manner, a wife can offer advice if she has another suggestion, but if the husband is not swayed, the wife must accept his authority and should comply, unless what he wants is unlawful or contrary to the teachings of Islam.

Both men and women have a higher obligation of obedience to Allāh (swt). The Messenger of Allāh (peace be upon him) said: "No obedience should ever be accepted to a created being which is in disobedience to Allāh, the Creator. O you, who spends her lifetime disobeying her Lord, no one amongst your enemies is wicked to you more than you are to yourself."

Often the breakdown of marriage is the feminist concept that "women and men are inherently of equal worth," and therefore the family can have two absolutely equal leaders, the wife and the husband.

If in the ensuing battle of wills, neither the husband or wife is ready to give way, so the result is will be divorce or separation, which will have negative results on the entire family, the sons and the daughters, and ultimately on the society at large. Righteous women most often understand that it is very natural for a husband to lead, provided that he leads in a wise and gentle manner.

It is one of the comforts of marriage for a wife to know that she does not have to take sole charge and responsibility for all decisions in the family. Allāh (swt) has created men and women equal in their essential dignity and human personhood, but different in function with male leadership in the home and in the family. Men and women complement one another and must never compete against each other. "But if a woman fears from her husband contempt or evasion, there is no sin upon them if they make terms of settlement between them - settlement is best. And present in [human] souls is stinginess. But if you do good and fear

Allāh - then indeed Allāh is ever, with what you
do, Acquainted." (4:128)

وَإِنِ ٱمْرَأَةٌ خَافَتْ مِنْ بَعْلِهَا نُشُوزًا أَوْ إِعْرَاضًا فَلَا جُنَاحَ عَلَيْهِمَآ
أَن يُصْلِحَا بَيْنَهُمَا صُلْحًا وَٱلصُّلْحُ خَيْرٌ وَأُحْضِرَتِ ٱلْأَنفُسُ ٱلشُّحَّ
وَإِن تُحْسِنُوا۟ وَتَتَّقُوا۟ فَإِنَّ ٱللَّهَ كَانَ بِمَا تَعْمَلُونَ
خَبِيرًا ۝

In every relationship a human being has –
whether with his parents, spouse, children,
neighbors, teachers, even (and especially) with
Allah Himself – there are "entrustments"
(amanat), rights or duties, he must fulfill in
order to do justice. Allah assures us that to act
justly is a "most excellent" thing to do. But He
also warns us with a subtlety that is not lost on
the conscious heart: if you choose not to act
with justice, and you instead violate the rights
you owe others, then know that God sees and
hears, and His perfect justice will eventually
bring you to task.

Do not live in the nightmares of the past or under the shade of what you have missed. Save yourself from the ghostly apparition of the past. You can never return the sun to its place of rising, the child to its mother's womb, milk to the udder, or tears to the eye? By constantly dwelling on the past and its happenings, you place yourself in a very sad and tragic state of mind.

Thinking and reading too much into the past is a waste of the present. When Allah mentioned the affairs of the previous nations, He, the Exalted, said: "That was a nation which has passed on. It will have [the consequence of] what it earned, and you will have what you have earned. And you will not be asked about what they used to do." (2:134)

تِلْكَ أُمَّةٌ قَدْ خَلَتْ لَهَا مَا كَسَبَتْ وَلَكُمْ مَّا كَسَبْتُمْ وَلَا تُسْأَلُونَ عَمَّا كَانُوا يَعْمَلُونَ ﴿١٣٤﴾

The former days are gone and done with, and you benefit nothing by carrying out an autopsy over them, by turning back the wheels of history. The person who lives in the past is like someone who tries to saw sawdust. Of old, they used to say: "Do not remove the dead from their graves."

There is no doubt that by putting Allah first in your quest for religious understanding and justice, you will find that the stress and tension in your heart, in your home will be replaced by love, light and the remembrance of Allah.

Those who believe, and whose hearts find satisfaction in the remembrance of Allah: for without doubt in the remembrance of Allah do hearts find satisfaction. (13:28)

ٱلَّذِينَ ءَامَنُواْ وَتَطۡمَئِنُّ قُلُوبُهُم بِذِكۡرِ ٱللَّهِ أَلَا بِذِكۡرِ ٱللَّهِ تَطۡمَئِنُّ ٱلۡقُلُوبُ ﴿٢٨﴾

The Family and the Home

Your home can be a beautiful oasis or a nightmare, depending on what you make of it. As the custodian of the home, the wife sets the tone and atmosphere of the household. The wife is not required by Islamic law to clean and cook, but she still the manager and therefore is responsible for ensuring that these essential jobs are done. If the husband can afford a maid or three, then he should hire a maid to relieve his wife of such tiring labor. However, if the husband cannot afford a maid, then the wife should contribute her own labor as a form of Sadaqah (charity) for which she will for certain receive a great reward from Allāh (swt). If you refuse to help your own family, then Allāh says: "Perhaps his Lord, if he divorces you, would substitute for him a wife better than you - submitting to Allāh, believing, devoutly obedient, repentant, worshipping, and traveling - [ones] previously married and virgins." (66:5)

عَسَىٰ رَبُّهُۥٓ إِن طَلَّقَكُنَّ أَن يُبْدِلَهُۥٓ أَزْوَٰجًا خَيْرًا مِّنكُنَّ مُسْلِمَٰتٍ مُّؤْمِنَٰتٍ قَٰنِتَٰتٍ تَٰٓئِبَٰتٍ عَٰبِدَٰتٍ سَٰٓئِحَٰتٍ ثَيِّبَٰتٍ وَأَبْكَارًا ۝

The wife who wants to keep the family happy and together must ensure that the home is a happy place to be in, physically mentally, and spiritually. The intelligent wife knows well the value of the personal touch around the house. She cooks and makes the house pleasant and filled with love. It is true that the way to a man's heart is through his stomach. Preparing good food has a very special blessing in Islam, whether it is for the family, a guest or for charity to the needy. If a wife is very busy to cook each day, then whatever food she makes with her own two hands, will earn her love and appreciation.

Sinan ibn Sannah reported: The Messenger of Allah, peace and blessings be upon him, said, "The one who eats gratefully an thankfully, has a reward similar to one who fasts patiently."

Lost are those who slay their children, without knowledge, and forbid food which Allāh hath provided for them, inventing (lies) against Allāh. They have indeed gone astray and heeded no guidance. (6:140)

قَدْ خَسِرَ ٱلَّذِينَ قَتَلُوٓاْ أَوْلَٰدَهُمْ سَفَهَاۢ بِغَيْرِ عِلْمٍ وَحَرَّمُواْ مَا رَزَقَهُمُ ٱللَّهُ ٱفْتِرَآءً عَلَى ٱللَّهِ قَدْ ضَلُّواْ وَمَا كَانُواْ مُهْتَدِينَ ﴿١٤٠﴾

Allāh says: "Eat from the good food and work righteousness. Indeed, I know of what you do."

The management of the household is not her only duty, the wife is also responsible for the early education and care of the children. Breast-feeding is also very vital, because of its physical benefits and for establishment of a close bond between baby and mother. Breast-milk shields the child from illness, and it helps a child's intellectual growth.

Allāh recommends a long period of breast-feeding to maximize the benefits to the child: "And We have enjoined upon man, to his parents, good treatment. His mother carried him with hardship and gave birth to him with hardship, and his gestation and *weaning [period] is thirty months*. [He grows] until, when he reaches maturity and reaches [the age of] forty years, he says, "My Lord, enable me to be grateful for Your favor which You have bestowed upon me and upon my parents and to work righteousness of which You will approve and make righteous for me my offspring." (46:15).

وَوَصَّيْنَا ٱلْإِنسَٰنَ بِوَٰلِدَيْهِ إِحْسَٰنًا حَمَلَتْهُ أُمُّهُۥ كُرْهًا وَوَضَعَتْهُ كُرْهًا وَحَمْلُهُۥ وَفِصَٰلُهُۥ ثَلَٰثُونَ شَهْرًا حَتَّىٰٓ إِذَا بَلَغَ أَشُدَّهُۥ وَبَلَغَ أَرْبَعِينَ سَنَةً قَالَ رَبِّ أَوْزِعْنِىٓ أَنْ أَشْكُرَ نِعْمَتَكَ ٱلَّتِىٓ أَنْعَمْتَ عَلَىَّ وَعَلَىٰ وَٰلِدَىَّ وَأَنْ أَعْمَلَ صَٰلِحًا تَرْضَىٰهُ وَأَصْلِحْ لِى فِى ذُرِّيَّتِىٓ إِنِّى تُبْتُ إِلَيْكَ وَإِنِّى مِنَ ٱلْمُسْلِمِينَ ﴿١٥﴾

The mother's care and love is of lasting significance. Positive childhood imprints are important to develop healthy adults. The effects of the impressions of child-hood remain throughout adult life. It is as "writing on stone"; its effects last forever. A wise mother can use positive influence to nurture her children to be good, loving, kind, confident, considerate, thoughtful, disciplined, intellectually, and spiritually awake and mindful of Allāh in whatever they do.

An Arab proverb says: "The mother is the school, the fountain of knowledge, the world, and with such tender solicitude for the child's future does this first and best teacher impart her." This is not an empty compliment but an important observation which has implications for the importance of the mother's job. From the moment of birth a child seeks to connect himself with his mother. Even most cats and animals do that. For many years the mother plays the most important role in his life.

The child is completely (100%) dependent upon her. It is in this environment that awareness, and ability to comprehend and cooperate first develops. The mother gives her child the first interaction with another human being. The mother is truly his first bridge to social life. A child who is not able to make a connection at all with his mother, or with some other person who took her place, would certainly perish. New situations happen each day. There are thousands of points in which a wife must apply her vision and understanding to her children's need. She can be very skillful only if she love her children and occupied in winning their affection and securing their welfare.

Human society is bound up with the attitude of a woman to motherhood. Women's part in life is often undervalued and treated as secondary. When the woman's part is undervalued, then the harmony of married life is destroyed.

If we can trace back the cases of failure in life, we would discover that the mother did not fulfil her function well. She did not give her children a good start. If the mother fails, if she is dissatisfied with her tasks and lack interest, then mankind is endangered.Islam has recognized the value and importance of motherhood. A mother is given full appreciation for her work and for the pains that she endures, and for the sacrifices that she makes for the sake of her children. The Messenger of Allāh, peace be upon him, said that Paradise lies at the feet of mothers."

Peace be upon him also said that: "I and the mothers whose face have grown dark (worrying and carrying about their children) shall be like this on the Day of Resurrection." The Prophet (peace be upon him) placed together his middle and forefingers (meaning, that the mothers would be standing next to him).

A man asked the Prophet, who is the most deserving? The Prophet replied: "Your mother." The man asked: "And who after that?" Peace be upon him said: "Your mother." The man asked: "And who after that?" Peace be upon him repeated: "Your mother, then your father, then your nearest relatives in order of closeness."

The father is also very important in child upbringing. However, it is wrong to devalue the role of the mother. Humans are obsessed with paid employment and material gains and so often the role of the homemaker and the mother has come to be regarded as meaningless. If a housewife or househusband is asked what they do (meaning their occupation) they likely to reply "Oh, not much at the moment. I stay at home and I take care of the children." Women and man have been brainwashed into thinking that a stay at home dad or mom is meaningless and demands no pay or special skill, and so their work is rated as zero in terms of occupational status and reward.

For both women and men their home must not be their prison. Their home must be the center of their attention and their partner and children's welfare must be their first priority after their obligation to Allāh. This must not rule out them taking on a job outside the home, or continuing with their education, or volunteering and helping the community. "Sallamah, the nurse of Ibrahim, the Prophet's son (before Ibrahim died), said to the Prophet (peace be upon him): O Messenger of Allāh, you brought good news of all the good things to men but not to women." Peace be upon him said: "Did your women friends asked you to ask me this question?" Sallamah said: "Yes, they did."

Peace be upon him said: "Does it not please anyone of you that if she becomes pregnant and her husband is happy with her that she receives the reward of one who fast and prays for the sake of Allāh? And when the labor and her pains come, no one in Heaven nor earth knows what is concealed in her womb to soothe her.

And when she delivers, not a mouthful of milk flows from her and not an instance of the baby's suck, but she receives, for every suck, the reward of a good deed. And if the baby kept her awake at night, she receives the reward of one who frees 70 slaves for the sake of Allāh." Do not be shaken by trials, tribulations, doubt, and hardships. Hardships strengthen the heart, atones for your sins, and helps to suppress an inclination towards pride and haughtiness. You might remember that in times of hardship you left senseless folly and you remembered Allah. When you were ill, tired, and afflicted, others extended sisterly and brotherly compassion to you, and you became the fortunate recipient of the supplications of the righteous. At such times, you willfully and humbly surrendered yourself to Allah's will and resigned yourself to His decree. Affliction begets circumspection and provides the afflicted with an early warning against following the wrong path. The one upon whom calamity has fallen can display courage with patience; and his circumstances, unlike the one who is drunk with worldly pleasures, permit him to solemnly prepare for a meeting with his Lord.

She is able to pass judgment on this world with an impartial ruling, and thus she will come to know it as something that is not worth pining for.

Other points associated with the wisdom and benefits of sometimes facing hardship, though they might escape our comprehension, are definitely present and known to the Lord of all that exists. So do not feel bad, for sadness will weaken your determination and the quality of your worship. One of the offshoots of depression is that it often causes one to be pessimistic, to find blame in everyone, including - and we seek refuge in Allah - Allah Himself. Sadness, grief, and anxiety are the roots of mental problems, the sources of stress. You have with you always the Quran, supplication, remembrance, and prayer. You can lighten the load of your anxiety by helping others and being productive. Do not surrender to sadness and pain by taking the easy path of idleness and inactivity, but pray, glorify Allah, read, write, work, visit relatives and friends, and reflect.

And your Lord says, "Call upon Me; I will respond to you." Indeed, those who disdain My worship will enter Hell [rendered] contemptible. (40:60)

وَقَالَ رَبُّكُمُ ٱدْعُونِىٓ أَسْتَجِبْ لَكُمْ إِنَّ ٱلَّذِينَ يَسْتَكْبِرُونَ عَنْ عِبَادَتِى سَيَدْخُلُونَ جَهَنَّمَ دَاخِرِينَ ٦٠

Call upon your Lord in humility and privately; indeed, He does not like transgressors. (7:55)

ٱدْعُوا۟ رَبَّكُمْ تَضَرُّعًا وَخُفْيَةً إِنَّهُۥ لَا يُحِبُّ ٱلْمُعْتَدِينَ ٥٥

So invoke Allah, [being] sincere to Him in religion, although the disbelievers dislike it. (40:14)

فَٱدْعُوا۟ ٱللَّهَ مُخْلِصِينَ لَهُ ٱلدِّينَ وَلَوْ كَرِهَ ٱلْكَٰفِرُونَ ١٤

Say, "Call upon Allah or call upon the Most Merciful. Whichever [name] you call - to Him belong the best names." And do not recite [too] loudly in your prayer or [too] quietly but seek between that an [intermediate] way. (17:110)

قُلِ ٱدْعُوا۟ ٱللَّهَ أَوِ ٱدْعُوا۟ ٱلرَّحْمَٰنَ ۖ أَيًّا مَّا تَدْعُوا۟ فَلَهُ ٱلْأَسْمَآءُ ٱلْحُسْنَىٰ ۚ وَلَا تَجْهَرْ بِصَلَاتِكَ وَلَا تُخَافِتْ بِهَا وَٱبْتَغِ بَيْنَ ذَٰلِكَ سَبِيلًا ﴿١١٠﴾

Acceptance of Good Advice

Leadership is defined as the process of influencing the activities of an organized group toward some goals. To achieve these goals, the leader must consult and accept good advice. In any successful marriage good communication between husband and wife is important. Matters about their children's education, marriage, and other family affairs such as money, must always be discussed for mutual agreement and understanding. The wife must also be concerned about her husband's work and other activities, and should keep up-to-date about current affairs and general knowledge. For this it helps a great deal if there is a reasonable level of educational quality between the wife and her husband. If the educational gap is too great, then they will be unable to communicate effectively because her degree of understanding will be too low for her to share his interests and worries.

The husband and wife could drift far apart since they have nothing in common or of shared interest to discuss. In such cases the husband may devote most of his free hours outside the home with his workmates, and comes home only to eat, wash, and sleep. If the wife is so unlucky to have a low educational level, then she must remedy the situation, whatever her age.

The Messenger of Allāh, peace and blessings be upon him, taught us that "the quest for knowledge is a duty for every person, female and male," and that it must be pursued and chased "from the cradle to the grave." The husband should try his best to support and to encourage her in every possible way. By broadening her knowledge, a woman becomes a better and a more interesting companion, and will be in a far better position to advise her partner. Similarly if her religious education was neglected at an earlier age, she can take classes, or she can read more books. This can help teach her own children in turn.

The best role model for an intellectual woman is the Prophet's wife Aisha who engaged the Prophet, peace and blessings be upon him, in deep questioning about Allāh until she was satisfied. As a result, Peace be upon him, advised people that they could learn from Aisha. Afterwards, when she became a widow, she became a noted authority on Hadith, and so her opinion was sought by many leaders on political, legal, and social issues. The wife and husband, at the time of marriage, may come from dissimilar backgrounds, different cultural, different socio-economic background, or simply a different family way of life. They must not react with fear to such natural differences but must exercise acceptance and humor in the process of adjustment. In this way, with time, they will come to a shared understanding and develop their own standards and sense of priorities. With time, they will begin to think of themselves as "we" instead of as two totally different and independent individuals.

Here are some verses from the Holy Quran about hope: O my sons, go and find out about Joseph and his brother and despair not of relief from Allah. Indeed, no one despairs of relief from Allah except the disbelieving people." (12:87)

يَـٰبَنِيَّ ٱذْهَبُواْ فَتَحَسَّسُواْ مِن يُوسُفَ وَأَخِيهِ وَلَا تَأَيْـَٔسُواْ مِن رَّوْحِ ٱللَّهِ ۖ إِنَّهُۥ لَا يَأْيْـَٔسُ مِن رَّوْحِ ٱللَّهِ إِلَّا ٱلْقَوْمُ ٱلْكَـٰفِرُونَ ﴿٨٧﴾

He said: "And who despairs of the mercy of his Lord except for those astray?" (15:56)

قَالَ وَمَن يَقْنَطُ مِن رَّحْمَةِ رَبِّهِۦٓ إِلَّا ٱلضَّآلُّونَ ﴿٥٦﴾

And cause not corruption upon the earth after its reformation. And invoke Him in fear and aspiration. Indeed, the mercy of Allah is near to the doers of good. (7:56)

وَلَا تُفْسِدُواْ فِي ٱلْأَرْضِ بَعْدَ إِصْلَـٰحِهَا وَٱدْعُوهُ خَوْفًا وَطَمَعًا ۚ إِنَّ رَحْمَتَ ٱللَّهِ قَرِيبٌ مِّنَ ٱلْمُحْسِنِينَ ﴿٥٦﴾

O Prophet! When ye do divorce women, divorce them at their prescribed periods, and count (accurately), their prescribed periods: And fear Allah your Lord: and turn them not out of their houses, nor shall they (themselves) leave, except in case they are guilty of some open lewdness, those are limits set by Allah: and any who transgresses the limits of Allah, does verily wrong his (own) soul: thou knowest not if perchance Allah will bring about thereafter some new situation. (65:1)

يَـٰٓأَيُّهَا ٱلنَّبِىُّ إِذَا طَلَّقْتُمُ ٱلنِّسَآءَ فَطَلِّقُوهُنَّ لِعِدَّتِهِنَّ وَأَحْصُوا۟ ٱلْعِدَّةَ وَٱتَّقُوا۟ ٱللَّهَ رَبَّكُمْ لَا تُخْرِجُوهُنَّ مِنۢ بُيُوتِهِنَّ وَلَا يَخْرُجْنَ إِلَّآ أَن يَأْتِينَ بِفَـٰحِشَةٍ مُّبَيِّنَةٍ وَتِلْكَ حُدُودُ ٱللَّهِ وَمَن يَتَعَدَّ حُدُودَ ٱللَّهِ فَقَدْ ظَلَمَ نَفْسَهُۥ لَا تَدْرِى لَعَلَّ ٱللَّهَ يُحْدِثُ بَعْدَ ذَٰلِكَ أَمْرًا ﴿١﴾

Allah is Subtle with His servants; He gives provisions to whom He wills. And He is the Powerful, the Exalted in Might. (42:19)

ٱللَّهُ لَطِيفٌۢ بِعِبَادِهِۦ يَرْزُقُ مَن يَشَآءُ وَهُوَ ٱلْقَوِىُّ ٱلْعَزِيزُ ﴿١٩﴾

Allah said: "My punishment - I afflict with it whom I will, but My mercy encompasses all things." So I will decree it [especially] for those who fear Me and give zakat and those who believe in Our verses. (7:156)

۞ وَٱكْتُبْ لَنَا فِى هَٰذِهِ ٱلدُّنْيَا حَسَنَةً وَفِى ٱلْأَخِرَةِ إِنَّا هُدْنَآ إِلَيْكَ قَالَ عَذَابِىٓ أُصِيبُ بِهِۦ مَنْ أَشَآءُ وَرَحْمَتِى وَسِعَتْ كُلَّ شَىْءٍ فَسَأَكْتُبُهَا لِلَّذِينَ يَتَّقُونَ وَيُؤْتُونَ ٱلزَّكَوٰةَ وَٱلَّذِينَ هُم بِـَٔايَٰتِنَا يُؤْمِنُونَ ﴿١٠٦﴾

[Remember] when you asked help of your Lord, and He answered you, "Indeed, I will reinforce you with a thousand from the angels, following one another." (8:9)

إِذْ تَسْتَغِيثُونَ رَبَّكُمْ فَٱسْتَجَابَ لَكُمْ أَنِّى مُمِدُّكُم بِأَلْفٍ مِّنَ ٱلْمَلَٰٓئِكَةِ مُرْدِفِينَ ﴿٩﴾

Never forget Allah, for He does not forget you ever. Allah is always with you, so do not ever feel alone.

Money

An important topic that needs understanding is money. Both husband and wife must support the family to the best of their abilities. If the wife does not work, then she must learn to live within the budget and show appreciation. "If you possessed the treasure of the Mercy of my Lord (wealth, money, provision, etc.), then you would surely hold back (from spending) for fear of (being exhausted), and man is ever miserly!" (17:100)

قُل لَّوۡ أَنتُمۡ تَمۡلِكُونَ خَزَآئِنَ رَحۡمَةِ رَبِّيٓ إِذًا لَّأَمۡسَكۡتُمۡ خَشۡيَةَ ٱلۡإِنفَاقِ وَكَانَ ٱلۡإِنسَٰنُ قَتُورًا ١٠٠

The sinner does not feel any remorse over his behavior and sins, this is because his heart is already dead. Those who are miserly and enjoin miserliness on other men and hide what Allah has bestowed upon them of His Bounties. And We have prepared for the disbelievers a disgraceful torment. (4:37)

$$ ٱلَّذِينَ يَبْخَلُونَ وَيَأْمُرُونَ ٱلنَّاسَ بِٱلْبُخْلِ وَيَكْتُمُونَ مَآ ءَاتَىٰهُمُ ٱللَّهُ مِن فَضْلِهِۦ ۗ وَأَعْتَدْنَا لِلْكَٰفِرِينَ عَذَابًا مُّهِينًا ٣٧ $$

And enjoin prayer upon your family [and people] and be steadfast therein. We ask you not for provision; We provide for you, and the [best] outcome is for [those of] righteousness. (20:132)

$$ وَأْمُرْ أَهْلَكَ بِٱلصَّلَوٰةِ وَٱصْطَبِرْ عَلَيْهَا ۖ لَا نَسْـَٔلُكَ رِزْقًا ۖ نَّحْنُ نَرْزُقُكَ ۗ وَٱلْعَٰقِبَةُ لِلتَّقْوَىٰ ١٣٢ $$

A woman must avoid the two extremes of meanness and extravagance as the Holy Quran states: "And [they are] those who, when they spend, do so not excessively or sparingly but are ever, between that, [justly] moderate." (25:67)

وَٱلَّذِينَ إِذَآ أَنفَقُواْ لَمۡ يُسۡرِفُواْ وَلَمۡ يَقۡتُرُواْ وَكَانَ بَيۡنَ ذَٰلِكَ قَوَامًا ﴿٦٧﴾

A wife must avoid all wastefulness, which the Quran identifies as a lack of gratitude to Allāh (swt). Indeed, the wasteful are brothers of the devils, and ever has Satan been to his Lord ungrateful. (17:27)

إِنَّ ٱلۡمُبَذِّرِينَ كَانُوٓاْ إِخۡوَٰنَ ٱلشَّيَٰطِينِۖ وَكَانَ ٱلشَّيۡطَٰنُ لِرَبِّهِۦ كَفُورًا ﴿٢٧﴾

Both husband and wife must also avoid demands for luxuries. If woman is a good wife, a husband may take pleasure in surprising his wife with gifts from time to time. However, to constantly buy clothes, jewelry, and cosmetics, can cause even patient husbands to feel tired and angry.

Allāh (swt) likes his servants to enjoy the lawful things, but in moderation. If man or woman has surplus it is best to give some of it away as sadaqah (charity) to people in need than to waste it.

If a wife earns money from anything, Allāh (swt) gave her full rights over that income. However, if her husband is not well off, it is the best act of charity to support her husband and to contribute something to the family expenses.

It is therefore best for a wife and husband to talk about money matters always from the start of the marriage. In this respect the family must identify the priorities, the highest amongst which must be to save enough money for the best education for the children, which the Messenger of Allāh (peace be upon him) described as the best gift one could make to their child.

If a person were given a choice between having status in society and plentiful money, and between having a happy, radiant, smiling self, one should choose the latter. For what is great wealth if it begets misery? And what is high position if what comes with it is constant gloominess? And what good is the most beautiful wife if she transforms her house into a fire? Much better than her - a thousand times at least - is a wife who has not reached such a pinnacle of beauty, but nonetheless has made her house a kind of paradise.

Consider this imagery: In a sense, the rose is smiling and so is the forest. The oceans, rivers, the sky, the stars and birds are all smiling. Similarly, the human being by his very nature is a smiling entity, were it not for those things that counteract this natural disposition, such as greed and selfishness, evils that contribute to his frowning. As such he is an anomaly and at odds with the natural harmony of all that surrounds him. Therefore the person whose heart is sullied cannot see things as they truly are.

Every person sees the world through himself-through his actions, thoughts, and motives. So if our actions are noble, if our thoughts are pure, and if our motives are honorable, then the spectacles through which we see the world will be clean, and the world will be seen by us as it really is a beautiful creation. If the eyes become dirty, and their lenses stained, then everything will seem to be black and morbid.

There are those souls that are able to turn everything into misery, whilst there are those that are able to derive happiness from the most difficult of circumstances. There is the woman whose eyes fall upon nothing but mistakes. Today is black because a piece of her jewelry got lost or because the maid put too much salt in the food. Then she flares up and curses, and no one in the house escapes from her wrath. Then there is the man who brings misery upon his own self and, through his disposition, heaps the same upon others. Any word that he hears he interprets in the worst possible way. He is affected gravely by the most insignificant of things that occur to him, or that have occurred to him through his actions.

He is drawn into misery by profits lost or by profits expected that went unrealized, and so on. The whole world from his perspective is black, and so he blackens it for those around him. Such people have much ability to over-exaggerate the trifles that occur to them. Thus they make mountains out of molehills. Their ability to do well is negligent, and they are never happy or content with that which they have, even if what they have is plenty. No matter how great their possessions, they will never feel any blessings from what they have. When he gave them from His bounty, they were stingy with it and turned away while they refused. (9:76)

فَلَمَّآ ءَاتَىٰهُم مِّن فَضْلِهِۦ بَخِلُواْ بِهِۦ وَتَوَلَّواْ وَّهُم مُّعْرِضُونَ ﴿٧٦﴾

[Those] who are stingy and enjoin upon people stinginess. And whoever turns away - then indeed, Allah is the Free of need, the Praiseworthy.

ٱلَّذِينَ يَبْخَلُونَ وَيَأْمُرُونَ ٱلنَّاسَ بِٱلْبُخْلِ وَمَن يَتَوَلَّ فَإِنَّ ٱللَّهَ هُوَ ٱلْغَنِيُّ ٱلْحَمِيدُ ﴿٢٤﴾

Friendship and Faith

The soul will never become pious and purified except through undergoing afflictions. It is the same as gold that can never be pure except after removing all the base metals in it. Allah has advised us to bear our trials and tribulations patiently. However, this is difficult without understanding that everything that happens in this world happens by the permission of Allah. No leaf falls from any tree without Allah's permission. No business crumbles, no horse stumbles, and no marriage ends without Allah's permission. No illness or injury touches a human being without Allah's permission. He has power over all things. Allah does what He does for reasons that are at times beyond our comprehension and for reasons that may or may not be apparent. However, Allah, in His infinite wisdom and mercy wants only what is best for us. Ultimately, what is best for us is eternal life in a place of eternal bliss, Paradise.

"Their Lord gives them glad tidings of a Mercy from Him, and that He is pleased (with them), and of Gardens (Paradise) for them wherein are everlasting delight." (9:21)

يُبَشِّرُهُمْ رَبُّهُم بِرَحْمَةٍ مِّنْهُ وَرِضْوَانٍ وَجَنَّاتٍ لَّهُمْ فِيهَا نَعِيمٌ مُّقِيمٌ ﴿٢١﴾

In the face of every trial, a believer must be certain that Allah does not decree for him anything but good. The good may be among the pleasures of this world or it may be in the hereafter. Prophet Muhammad, peace be upon him, said: "How wonderful is the affair of the believer, for his affairs are all good. If something good happens to him, he is thankful for it and that is good for him. If something bad happens to him, he bears it with patience and that is also good for him." Allah tests us with the trials and tribulations of life, and if we bear patiently we will attain great reward. Through changing circumstances and trying times Allah tests our level of faith, ascertains our ability to be patient and wipes away some of our sins. Allah is all loving and wise and knows us better than we know ourselves.

We will not attain Paradise without His mercy and His mercy is manifest in the tests and trials of this life. The life of this world is mere deception. The most beneficial thing to us are the good deeds that we were able to perform. Families are a trial, for Allah says that they can lead us astray, but equally they can lead us to Paradise. Wealth is a trial; coveting it can make us greedy and miserly, but distributing it and using it to benefit those in need can bring us closer to Allah. Health is also a trial. Good health can make us feel invincible and not in need of Allah, but bad health has a way of humbling us and forcing us to depend on God. How a believer reacts to the circumstances of life is very important.

What happens if the pleasures of this life suddenly become torments? How should one behave when struck by illness or injury? Of course, we accept our fate and try to bear the pain, sadness, or suffering patiently because we know with certainty that from this Allah will bring about much good.

Prophet Muhammad, peace be upon him, said:
"No misfortune or disease befalls a Muslim, no
worry or grief or harm or distress — not even
a thorn that pricks him, but Allah will expiate
for some of his sins because of that." However,
we are imperfect human beings. We can read
these words, we can even understand the
sentiment, but behaving with acceptance is
sometimes very difficult. It is much easier to
bemoan and cry about our situation, but our
Most Merciful has given us clear guidelines and
promised us two things, if we worship Him and
follow His guidance we will be rewarded with
Paradise and that after hardship comes ease.
"So verily, with the hardship, there is relief."
(94:5)

فَإِنَّ مَعَ ٱلْعُسْرِ يُسْرًا ٥

A believer is obligated to look after his body
and mind, therefore trying to maintain good
health is essential. However, when struck by
illness or injury, it is vital to follow Allah's
guidance.

A believer must seek medical aid and do everything he can to bring about a cure or recovery, but at the same time he must seek help through prayer, remembrance of God and acts of worship. Islam is a holistic way of life, both physical and spiritual health go hand in hand. In part two we will examine in more detail the steps to take when struck by illness or injury.

Friendship

A friend should be more than just a person who you can hang out with at any time – they should be a confidante and someone who can always give you the right advice no matter what. The relationship kept with friends is stressed very highly in Islam. Not only is it encouraged, but the importance of having good friends and surrounding yourself with good company is relayed to Muslims many a time. Before marriage a woman naturally has a circle of friends. These friendships are often for life and not let go on marriage, but a wife must remember that her closet friend should always be her partner, her husband.

It is wrong to tell her friends the details of her married life, or to discuss the sexual relationship. It must always remain entirely private. She must never talk to anyone about what her husband says to her in a private conversation. It is reckless and could do harm if his private remarks become a source of gossip. If a wife cannot control her own tongue, she will lose her husband. If she wants to be her husband's ally, then she must always keep confidential matters to herself. "Do they not know that Allāh knows what they keep secret and what they make known?" (2:77)

أَوَلَا يَعْلَمُونَ أَنَّ ٱللَّهَ يَعْلَمُ مَا يُسِرُّونَ وَمَا يُعْلِنُونَ ﴿٧٧﴾

"Do they think that Allāh hears not their secrets and their private conversations? Yes, [We do], and Our messengers are with them recording." (43:80)

أَمْ يَحْسَبُونَ أَنَّا لَا نَسْمَعُ سِرَّهُمْ وَنَجْوَىٰهُم بَلَىٰ وَرُسُلُنَا لَدَيْهِمْ يَكْتُبُونَ ﴿٨٠﴾

"Verily Allāh knows the secrets of the heavens and the earth: and Allāh Sees well all that ye do." (49:18)

إِنَّ ٱللَّهَ يَعْلَمُ غَيْبَ ٱلسَّمَوَٰتِ وَٱلْأَرْضِ وَٱللَّهُ بَصِيرٌ بِمَا تَعْمَلُونَ ﴿١٨﴾

And when the Prophet confided to one of his wives, but she told others of it and Allāh showed it to him, he made known part of it and ignored a part. And when he informed her about it, she said: "Who told you this?" He said, "I was informed by the Knowing, the Acquainted." (66:33)

وَإِذْ أَسَرَّ ٱلنَّبِيُّ إِلَىٰ بَعْضِ أَزْوَاجِهِ حَدِيثًا فَلَمَّا نَبَّأَتْ بِهِ وَأَظْهَرَهُ ٱللَّهُ عَلَيْهِ عَرَّفَ بَعْضَهُ وَأَعْرَضَ عَنْ بَعْضٍ فَلَمَّا نَبَّأَهَا بِهِ قَالَتْ مَنْ أَنْبَأَكَ هَٰذَا قَالَ نَبَّأَنِيَ ٱلْعَلِيمُ ٱلْخَبِيرُ ﴿٣﴾

If there is ever an issue between her and her husband on which she needs advice, she must be very cautious, and must ask only a person of proven integrity, who will give her good and sincere counsel, and will never tell others.

In her public appearance, a woman must always observe Islamic codes of dress and behave modesty. She must not show off her figure, her clothes and her jewelry. She must also avoid wearing perfume in public. The perfume is only to attract her husband. Her dress must cover all parts of the body except her face and hands. It must not be tight nor transparent. It must not make her look like a man. The style and color is not important as long as the dress conforms to the Islamic values, and is not designed to attract men's attention. When she is in her own house, or away from the sight of men, she may dress in anything that she likes to please herself and her husband. And tell the believing women to reduce [some] of their vision and guard their private parts and not expose their adornment except that which appears thereof and to wrap [a portion of] their headcovers over their chests and not expose their adornment except to their husbands, their fathers, their husbands' fathers, their sons, their husbands' sons, their brothers, their brothers' sons, their sisters' sons, their women, that which their right hands possess, or those male attendants having no physical desire, or children who are not yet aware of the private aspects of women. And let them not stamp their feet to make known what they conceal of their adornment. And turn to Allāh in repentance, all of you, O believers that you might succeed. (24:31)

وَقُل لِّلْمُؤْمِنَٰتِ يَغْضُضْنَ مِنْ أَبْصَٰرِهِنَّ وَيَحْفَظْنَ فُرُوجَهُنَّ وَلَا يُبْدِينَ زِينَتَهُنَّ إِلَّا مَا ظَهَرَ مِنْهَا وَلْيَضْرِبْنَ بِخُمُرِهِنَّ عَلَىٰ جُيُوبِهِنَّ وَلَا يُبْدِينَ زِينَتَهُنَّ إِلَّا لِبُعُولَتِهِنَّ أَوْ ءَابَآئِهِنَّ أَوْ ءَابَآءِ بُعُولَتِهِنَّ أَوْ أَبْنَآئِهِنَّ أَوْ أَبْنَآءِ بُعُولَتِهِنَّ أَوْ إِخْوَٰنِهِنَّ أَوْ بَنِىٓ إِخْوَٰنِهِنَّ أَوْ بَنِىٓ أَخَوَٰتِهِنَّ أَوْ نِسَآئِهِنَّ أَوْ مَا مَلَكَتْ أَيْمَٰنُهُنَّ أَوِ التَّٰبِعِينَ غَيْرِ أُو۟لِى الْإِرْبَةِ مِنَ الرِّجَالِ أَوِ الطِّفْلِ الَّذِينَ لَمْ يَظْهَرُوا۟ عَلَىٰ عَوْرَٰتِ النِّسَآءِ وَلَا يَضْرِبْنَ بِأَرْجُلِهِنَّ لِيُعْلَمَ مَا يُخْفِينَ مِن زِينَتِهِنَّ وَتُوبُوٓا۟ إِلَى اللَّهِ جَمِيعًا أَيُّهَ الْمُؤْمِنُونَ لَعَلَّكُمْ تُفْلِحُونَ ٣١

Life is like an art or a science: it needs to be learned and cultivated. If you wish to mention the faults of your friend, mention your own faults first. Your best friend should be the one who: seeing her reminds you of Allah, speaking to her increases your knowledge, and her actions remind you of the hereafter. It is much better for a person to plant love in her life than to destroy others. Most people do not open their eyes to the beauty of 1ife, but open them only to gold or silver. They pass by a lush and luxuriant garden, a beautiful bed of roses, a flowing river, or a group of singing birds, yet they are unmoved by such scenes. Our body has been equipped with eyes to see beauty with, yet we have trained them to look on nothing but what we cannot have. Nothing causes the soul or the face to frown more often and with more intensity than despondency. If you want to be a smiling person, then wage war with despondency and hopelessness. The door to opportunity is often open to you and to others, and so is the door to success. So indoctrinate your mind with hopes of prosperity in the future.

If you believe that you are inconsequential and have been created for things of only minor importance, then your achievement in life will never surpass this initial goal. And if you believe that your calling in life is to achieve extraordinary feats, then you will feel in you a determination that can destroy all kinds of barriers. The soul gives resolution and will power in proportion to your goal. Hence you must identify your goal, and let it be high and difficult to achieve. Never feel despondency as long as every day you are taking a new step in its direction. What blocks the soul, making it frown and placing it in a dark prison? The answer is despondency, hopelessness, seeing everything as being evil, searching for faults in friends and others and regularly speaking about the evilness of the world.

The wisdom behind the difference between a woman's public and private appearance

A woman's outer beauty is a part of her sexual appeal. And dress and adornment can either enhance that attraction or can conceal it. Allāh requires a husband and wife to be faithful to each other, and He recommended punishment for adultery. It is a part of wisdom then to fear Allāh and to wear clothes that conceal the body, so as not to encourage the very thing which Allāh forbids. On the other hand, Allāh does not regard sexual relations between spouses as sinful. On the contrary, Allāh wants married partners to enjoy sexual relations with each other since this will reduce temptations to seek satisfaction outside marriage. Therefore, women at home must take care of their appearance and should wear nice clothes, jewelry and perfume to enhance their attraction to their husband.

"O Prophet! Why do you forbid (yourself) that which Allāh has made lawful for you; you seek to please your wives; and Allāh is Forgiving, Merciful. ((66:1)

$$\text{يَٰٓأَيُّهَا ٱلنَّبِىُّ لِمَ تُحَرِّمُ مَآ أَحَلَّ ٱللَّهُ لَكَ تَبْتَغِى مَرْضَاتَ أَزْوَٰجِكَ وَٱللَّهُ غَفُورٌ رَّحِيمٌ ﴿١﴾}$$

Most wives foolishly practice the reverse, they wear their most attractive clothes outside the house, in order to be admired by strangers, and when they are at home they wear their old and dirty clothes with untidy hair and appearance as if it no longer matters if their own husbands find them attractive or not. The Messenger of Allāh, peace and blessings be upon him, said that all women may go out alone for their needs. However, provided they are in hijab (modest Islamic dress), then they may go out for any lawful purpose.

Women however must not roam around aimlessly and must not mix without cause with men. They should always tell their husbands where they are going and have their consent. Women must also not put themselves in a situation where they are alone with men other than their husbands, fathers, or brothers (within the prohibited degrees of marriage).

Women must not allow into their homes men of whom Allāh and their husbands would not approve, nor should they visit such men. There may also be women of whom the husband disapproves, maybe because of their bad habits of spreading gossip, or maybe because they interfere in the family's affairs, or because of other harmful influence.

Women must avoid situations or actions that could give rise to gossip about their conduct, or jealousy of their husbands, even if they have no bad intentions.

If a woman's appearance and behavior indicate that she is a faithful wife, she will gain the respect of her husband, other people and avoid unwanted attention. If the husband is certain of his wife's true respect and love for him, he will trust her always, and be spared from jealousy and suspicion. All these principles of conduct, strengths the marriage and the success of the family's life.

Other aspects of family and social life that a wife must observe are respect for her parents and her husband's family. She must also be a good mother and a kind neighbor.

Worship Allāh and associate nothing with Him, and to parents do good, and to relatives, orphans, the needy, the near neighbor, the neighbor farther away, the companion at your side, the traveler, and those whom your right hands possess. Indeed, Allāh does not like those who are self-deluding and boastful. (4:36)

۞ وَٱعْبُدُواْ ٱللَّهَ وَلَا تُشْرِكُواْ بِهِۦ شَيْـًٔا وَبِٱلْوَٰلِدَيْنِ إِحْسَٰنًا وَبِذِى ٱلْقُرْبَىٰ وَٱلْيَتَٰمَىٰ وَٱلْمَسَٰكِينِ وَٱلْجَارِ ذِى ٱلْقُرْبَىٰ وَٱلْجَارِ ٱلْجُنُبِ وَٱلصَّاحِبِ بِٱلْجَنۢبِ وَٱبْنِ ٱلسَّبِيلِ وَمَا مَلَكَتْ أَيْمَٰنُكُمْ إِنَّ ٱللَّهَ لَا يُحِبُّ مَن كَانَ مُخْتَالًا فَخُورًا ٣٦

And if any one of the polytheists seeks your protection, then grant him protection so that he may hear the words of Allāh. Then deliver him to his place of safety. That is because they are a people who do not know. (9:6)

وَإِنْ أَحَدٌ مِّنَ ٱلْمُشْرِكِينَ ٱسْتَجَارَكَ فَأَجِرْهُ حَتَّىٰ يَسْمَعَ كَلَٰمَ ٱللَّهِ ثُمَّ أَبْلِغْهُ مَأْمَنَهُۥ ذَٰلِكَ بِأَنَّهُمْ قَوْمٌ لَّا يَعْلَمُونَ ٦

Allāh, Merciful said: "Never will I allow to be lost the work of [any] worker among you, whether male or female; you are of one another. So those who emigrated or were evicted from their homes or were harmed in My cause or fought or were killed - I will surely remove from them their misdeeds, and I will surely admit them to gardens beneath which rivers flow as reward from Allāh , and Allāh has with Him the best reward." (3:195)

فَٱسْتَجَابَ لَهُمْ رَبُّهُمْ أَنِّى لَآ أُضِيعُ عَمَلَ عَامِلٍ مِّنكُم مِّن ذَكَرٍ أَوْ أُنثَىٰ بَعْضُكُم مِّنۢ بَعْضٍ فَٱلَّذِينَ هَاجَرُواْ وَأُخْرِجُواْ مِن دِيَٰرِهِمْ وَأُوذُواْ فِى سَبِيلِى وَقَٰتَلُواْ وَقُتِلُواْ لَأُكَفِّرَنَّ عَنْهُمْ سَيِّـَٔاتِهِمْ وَلَأُدْخِلَنَّهُمْ جَنَّٰتٍ تَجْرِى مِن تَحْتِهَا ٱلْأَنْهَٰرُ ثَوَابًا مِّنْ عِندِ ٱللَّهِ وَٱللَّهُ عِندَهُۥ حُسْنُ ٱلثَّوَابِ ﴿١٩٥﴾

The Prophet, peace be upon him, said: "Be mindful of Allah, you shall find Him in front of you. Know Allah in times of prosperity so He will know you in times of hardship. Know that whatever passed you by could never have happened, and what happened could never have been avoided. Know that victory comes with patience, relief comes with affliction, and with hardship comes ease."

So always remember the favors of Allah upon you and how they surround you from above and below, indeed, from every direction. Allah gave you from all you asked of Him. And if you should count the favor of Allah, you could not count them. Indeed, mankind is generally most unjust and ungrateful (14:34)

وَءَاتَـٰكُم مِّن كُلِّ مَا سَأَلْتُمُوهُ وَإِن تَعُدُّوا نِعْمَتَ اللَّهِ لَا تُحْصُوهَآ إِنَّ الْإِنسَـٰنَ لَظَلُومٌ كَفَّارٌ ۝

Children, health, safety, nourishment, clothing, air, and water these all point to the world being yours, yet you do not realize it. You enjoy all that life has to offer, you have at your disposal beautiful eyes, ears, a tongue, lips, two hands, and two legs, yet remain ungrateful. Do you not see that Allah has made subject to you whatever is in the heavens and whatever is in the earth and amply bestowed upon you His favors, [both] apparent and unapparent? But of the people is he who disputes about Allah without knowledge or guidance or an enlightening Book [from Him]. (31:20)

أَلَمْ تَرَوْا أَنَّ ٱللَّهَ سَخَّرَ لَكُم مَّا فِى ٱلسَّمَٰوَٰتِ وَمَا فِى ٱلْأَرْضِ وَأَسْبَغَ عَلَيْكُمْ نِعَمَهُۥ ظَٰهِرَةً وَبَاطِنَةً وَمِنَ ٱلنَّاسِ مَن يُجَٰدِلُ فِى ٱللَّهِ بِغَيْرِ عِلْمٍ وَلَا هُدًى وَلَا كِتَٰبٍ مُّنِيرٍ ٢٠

So which of the favors of your Lord would you deny? (55: 13)

فَبِأَيِّ ءَالَآءِ رَبِّكُمَا تُكَذِّبَانِ ١٣

Can you picture yourself walking without feet? Should you take it lightly that you sleep soundly while misery hinders the sleep of many? Should you forget that you fill stomach with delicious food and cool water while the pleasure of good food and drink is impossible for many, due to sickness and disease? And consider the gifts of hearing and seeing with which you have been given. Look at your healthy skin and be grateful that you have been saved from viruses that attack it. And reflect on your ability to think and reason while others suffer from mental diseases. Would you sell your ability to see and hear for the weight of Mount Uhud in gold, or your ability to speak for 100,000 camels?

Allah has given you many gifts, yet you remain ungrateful. And also in your ownselves. Will you not then see? (51:21)

وَفِىٓ أَنفُسِكُمۡ أَفَلَا تُبۡصِرُونَ ٢١

You think about what you do not have and are ungrateful for what you have been given. You are troubled by a loss of some wealth, yet you have the keys to happiness and many blessings. Reflect upon yourself, your family, your friends, and the entire world that is around you. They recognize the Grace of Allah, yet they deny it and most of them are disbelievers (deny the Prophethood of Muhammad, peace and blessings be upon him). 16: 83)

يَعۡرِفُونَ نِعۡمَتَ ٱللَّهِ ثُمَّ يُنكِرُونَهَا وَأَكۡثَرُهُمُ ٱلۡكَٰفِرُونَ ٨٣

The Sexual Relationship

According to Islam, sexuality is a natural part of our identity as human beings. For Muslims, sexual relations are allowed within a marriage between a wife and husband. Marriage is much more than sex, but the sexual relationship is important. Because without a good sexual relationship, it is likely that the husband or wife could look somewhere else for love and emotional or physical fulfilment. The husband and wife need to be kind and responsive to each other's needs and moods. Women (and indeed, men) frequently fail to understand and see the differences between female and male sexuality and so they offend each other. They should always make clear to one another what they dislike or like. The wife should take care of herself always and should make herself more attractive to her husband. Allāh has encouraged the expression of love in the context of a lawful and spiritual relationship.

"Your wives are a place of sowing of seed for you, so come to your place of cultivation however you wish and put forth [righteousness] for yourselves. And fear Allāh and know that you will meet Him. And give good tidings to the believers. (2:223)

نِسَآؤُكُمْ حَرْثٌ لَّكُمْ فَأْتُواْ حَرْثَكُمْ أَنَّىٰ شِئْتُمْ وَقَدِّمُواْ لِأَنفُسِكُمْ وَاتَّقُواْ اللَّهَ وَاعْلَمُوٓاْ أَنَّكُم مُّلَـٰقُوهُ وَبَشِّرِ الْمُؤْمِنِينَ ﴿٢٢٣﴾

If a wife is not feeling well or has good reasons for not wanting sex, the husband must understand but she must not make a habit of refusing him. Women often underestimate the humiliation a husband feels if he is often rejected. The Prophet, peace and blessing be upon him, said: "When a woman who has been called to her husband's bed but she refuses, if he spends the night feeling bad, the angels will curse her until the morning."

This is very tough language, but it must be said. There is serious consequences of their constant refusal. Because a man who is frequently rejected by his wife will feel offended, frustrated, and depressed. This will cause big tension and problems in the marriage and can lead to divorce. A patient man often will not say or pursue unlawful gratifications somewhere else, but some men will search for satisfaction elsewhere, with a prostitute or mistress, or by taking another wife secretly.

An intelligent wife that loves her husband must understand the possible consequences of her coldness and must give her husband all the love he wants. In a long Hadith from Sahih Muslim, it said that some of the Prophet's Companions noticed that rich people might get more reward from Allāh because of their ability to give more charity. The Prophet, peace be upon him, said that Allāh (swt) made other things to be given in charity.

For example, praising Allāh, enjoining of good actions, forbidding of evil actions, and sexual relations. The Companions said: "When one of us fulfils his sexual desire will we have reward for that?" Peace be upon him said: "If a person does it unlawfully he would be sinning. But if he does it lawfully, with his wife, he will have a reward."

Therefore, if a wife satisfies her husband within the lawful framework of marriage and so protecting him (and herself) from unlawful acts, then not only this pleases her husband but this pleases Allāh (swt) greatly. "It has been made permissible for you the night preceding fasting to go to your wives [for sexual relations]. They are clothing for you and you are clothing for them. Allāh knows that you used to deceive yourselves, so He accepted your repentance and forgave you. So now, have relations with them and seek that which Allāh has decreed for you.

And eat and drink until the white thread of dawn becomes distinct to you from the black thread [of night]. Then complete the fast until the sunset. And do not have relations with them as long as you are staying for worship in the mosques. These are the limits [set by] Allāh, so do not approach them. Thus does Allāh make clear His ordinances to the people that they may become righteous." (2:187)

أُحِلَّ لَكُمْ لَيْلَةَ ٱلصِّيَامِ ٱلرَّفَثُ إِلَىٰ نِسَآئِكُمْ هُنَّ لِبَاسٌ لَّكُمْ وَأَنتُمْ لِبَاسٌ لَّهُنَّ عَلِمَ ٱللَّهُ أَنَّكُمْ كُنتُمْ تَخْتَانُونَ أَنفُسَكُمْ فَتَابَ عَلَيْكُمْ وَعَفَا عَنكُمْ فَٱلْـَٰٔنَ بَٰشِرُوهُنَّ وَٱبْتَغُوا۟ مَا كَتَبَ ٱللَّهُ لَكُمْ وَكُلُوا۟ وَٱشْرَبُوا۟ حَتَّىٰ يَتَبَيَّنَ لَكُمُ ٱلْخَيْطُ ٱلْأَبْيَضُ مِنَ ٱلْخَيْطِ ٱلْأَسْوَدِ مِنَ ٱلْفَجْرِ ثُمَّ أَتِمُّوا۟ ٱلصِّيَامَ إِلَى ٱلَّيْلِ وَلَا تُبَٰشِرُوهُنَّ وَأَنتُمْ عَٰكِفُونَ فِى ٱلْمَسَٰجِدِ تِلْكَ حُدُودُ ٱللَّهِ فَلَا تَقْرَبُوهَا كَذَٰلِكَ يُبَيِّنُ ٱللَّهُ ءَايَٰتِهِۦ لِلنَّاسِ لَعَلَّهُمْ يَتَّقُونَ ﴿١٨٧﴾

The right to sex is of course reciprocal. The wife also has the same rights over her husband. It should also be mentioned here again that Allāh wants you to have children. Allāh, the Merciful, said: "So now have sexual relations with them, and seek that which Allāh has ordained for you." (2:187)

Islam has not prohibited child spacing by science that do not have any harmful side effects, but if it is with mutual consent of wife and husband.

Jabir, a good Companion of the Prophet, peace be upon him, said that during the period when the Holy Quran was being revealed, people practiced contraception by Coitus interrupts (azl). Also known as the pull-out method, is a method of birth control in which a man, during sexual intercourse, withdraws his penis from a woman's vagina prior to orgasm.

Muslim added that the Prophet, peace be upon him, heard about Azl, but did not prohibit it. Abortion however is prohibited unless the mother's life is at stake. This applies also to forms of family planning which allow conception to take place but kill the embryo or prevent it from settling in the womb. Barrier methods such as the condom are closest to the hadith (i.e., azl). Natural methods such as checking body temperature to avoid sex round the time of ovulation are good alternatives.

Women and men should pay attention to personal cleanliness so as not to cause offence. The wife must always bathe, and she should use effective deodorants. She should also remove pubic hair and use pleasant perfume to please her husband. Having and raising a child is important, however sex is not only intended for reproduction. Sex within marriage is to create tenderness between two people. Sex between two people who are married is a form of worship which they will be rewarded for.

The Prophet, peace be upon him, spoke about the importance of foreplay and speaking to partners in loving terms. He advised husbands to take care that their wives achieve orgasm and enjoy intimacy. However, anal sex is forbidden.

Again, Islam does not allow men or women to have sex outside of marriage. The reason for this is that there can be negative consequences in having pre-marital sex. Some of the consequences can include things such as unwanted pregnancies, sexually transmitted infections and negative impact on family relationships. Because the process that leads to physical attraction and sexual intimacy is part of human nature, Muslims are advised to avoid circumstances that could result in sex outside marriage. With regards to masturbation, there are different many views on whether it is allowed or forbidden. Most Islamic schools of thought take the view that masturbation is forbidden or at least disliked, however they allow it to take place when it is considered a necessity.

For example, someone who is unmarried could masturbate as a last resort as a way of avoiding having sex outside of marriage. However, masturbation is not acceptable during daylight hours in Ramadan because it is seen as breaking the fast.

In Islam having children is encouraged and they are considered a gift from Allah. However women are allowed to decide for themselves whether or not they want a child. Within Islam, abortion is not considered acceptable unless the mother's life is endangered. Her life is considered to be more significant than that of her embryo if her life or health is put at risk by the pregnancy. In this situation her position in the family is more important than the potential of life residing within the embryo. This is the only circumstance where termination is lawful within Islam. A belief that the soul does not enter the fetus until the 40th day of gestation indicates that an abortion should be carried out before this time.

Allah's Messenger, peace be upon him, said: "(The matter of the Creation of) a human being is put together in the womb of the mother in *40 days*, and then he becomes a clot of thick blood for a similar period, and then a piece of flesh for a similar period. Then Allah sends an angel who is ordered to write four things. He is ordered to write down his (i.e. the new creature's) deeds, his livelihood, his (date of) death, and whether he will be blessed or wretched (in religion). Then the soul is breathed into him. So, a man amongst you may do (good deeds till there is only a cubit between him and Paradise and then what has been written for him decides his behavior and he starts doing (evil) deeds characteristic of the people of the (Hell) Fire. And similarly a man amongst you may do (evil) deeds till there is only a cubit between him and the (Hell) Fire, and then what has been written for him decides his behavior, and he starts doing deeds characteristic of the people of Paradise."

"Verily, the creation of one of you is brought together in the mother's womb for forty days in the form of a drop (nutfah), then he becomes a clot ('alaqah) for a like period, then a lump for a like period, then there is sent an angel who blows the soul into him." — Hadith #4, Imam al-Nawawī's Forty Hadith, Ibn Hajar al-Haytamī, al-Fath al-mubīn sharh al

The Quran does not explicitly refer to abortion but offers guidance on related matters. Many scholars accept that this guidance can properly be applied to abortion. The Quran states: "Whosoever has spared the life of a soul, it is as though he has spared the life of all people. Whosoever has killed a soul, it is as though he has murdered all of mankind." (5:32)

مِنْ أَجْلِ ذَٰلِكَ كَتَبْنَا عَلَىٰ بَنِىٓ إِسْرَٰٓءِيلَ أَنَّهُۥ مَن قَتَلَ نَفْسًۢا بِغَيْرِ نَفْسٍ أَوْ فَسَادٍ فِى ٱلْأَرْضِ فَكَأَنَّمَا قَتَلَ ٱلنَّاسَ جَمِيعًا وَمَنْ أَحْيَاهَا فَكَأَنَّمَآ أَحْيَا ٱلنَّاسَ جَمِيعًا ۚ وَلَقَدْ جَآءَتْهُمْ رُسُلُنَا بِٱلْبَيِّنَٰتِ ثُمَّ إِنَّ كَثِيرًا مِّنْهُم بَعْدَ ذَٰلِكَ فِى ٱلْأَرْضِ لَمُسْرِفُونَ ۝٣٢

Islam recognizes that lifelong marriage is not always possible and provides laws for divorce. Divorce is accepted and referred to as talaq. Sometimes people think that a married Muslim man can divorce his wife simply by saying talaq three times, however this is a controversial practice and is against the teachings of Islam. In Islam, Marriage is a sacred bond and divorce should only be used as a last resort. If a wife and husband are having marriage difficulties, as a first step they should appoint mediators to resolve the conflict. If this does not work, then either the husband or wife can ask for a divorce.

A wife can ask her husband to divorce her, and if the husband refuses, she can go to an Islamic court to ask for a divorce. A man can divorce his wife following a procedure set by Islamic law. The man must claim that he wants to divorce his wife three times, within a three-month period. After getting divorced, the man is required to financially support the woman and his children.

Islam has clear and explicit rules regarding sex and sexuality. Sex is only allowed within a marriage, and an Islamic marriage can only take place between a man and a woman. Islam does not allow sex before marriage or for people to have anal sex. These rules apply equally for both straight and gay people. If someone does have feelings of attraction towards members of the same sex, this is not considered sinful. However, acting on these feelings is a great sin that leads to the hellfire and eternal damnation. In Islam, having thoughts or feelings which are against the teachings of Islam is not a sin, it is only your voluntary actions which can be a sin.

Muslims who are attracted to members of the same sex are expected to resist their desires and struggle against them. Struggling to keep your desires in check for the sake of Allah's pleasure is considered jihad bin nafs, a sacred struggle against ones ego. The person who does this successfully receives spiritual illumination and a great reward and honor in the eyes of Allah.

[He] who created death and life to test you [as to] which of you is best in deed - and He is the Exalted in Might, the Forgiving. (67:2)

ٱلَّذِى خَلَقَ ٱلْمَوْتَ وَٱلْحَيَوٰةَ لِيَبْلُوَكُمْ أَيُّكُمْ أَحْسَنُ عَمَلًا وَهُوَ ٱلْعَزِيزُ ٱلْغَفُورُ ﴿٢﴾

And We will surely test you with something of fear and hunger and a loss of wealth and lives and fruits, but give good tidings to the patient. (2:155)

وَلَنَبْلُوَنَّكُم بِشَىْءٍ مِّنَ ٱلْخَوْفِ وَٱلْجُوعِ وَنَقْصٍ مِّنَ ٱلْأَمْوَٰلِ وَٱلْأَنفُسِ وَٱلثَّمَرَٰتِ وَبَشِّرِ ٱلصَّٰبِرِينَ ﴿١٥٥﴾

Do you think that you will enter Paradise before Allah tests those of you who fought (in His Cause) and (also) tests those who are As-Sabirin (the patient ones, etc.)? (3:142)

أَمْ حَسِبْتُمْ أَن تَدْخُلُوا ٱلْجَنَّةَ وَلَمَّا يَعْلَمِ ٱللَّهُ ٱلَّذِينَ جَٰهَدُوا مِنكُمْ وَيَعْلَمَ ٱلصَّٰبِرِينَ ﴿١٤٢﴾

Asking Allah for Forgiveness

Allah says in the Quran: "Say: O my Servants who have transgressed against their souls! Despair not of the Mercy of Allah: for Allah forgives all sins: for He is Oft-Forgiving, Most Merciful." [39:53]

قُلْ يَٰعِبَادِيَ ٱلَّذِينَ أَسْرَفُوا۟ عَلَىٰٓ أَنفُسِهِمْ لَا تَقْنَطُوا۟ مِن رَّحْمَةِ ٱللَّهِ إِنَّ ٱللَّهَ يَغْفِرُ ٱلذُّنُوبَ جَمِيعًا إِنَّهُۥ هُوَ ٱلْغَفُورُ ٱلرَّحِيمُ ٥٣

This verse speaks about those who repent. It tells us that any sin, no matter how major, can be expiated by sincere and proper repentance. The conditions for repentance are as follows:

- The penitent person desist from the sinful act.
- He feels deep and genuine regret for having committed the sin.
- He resolve, in his heart, never to return to the sin again.
- Finally, if the sin caused a transgression against the rights of another person, he needs to do his best to make amends.

When Allah sees this sincere repentance from one of His servants – a servant who truly turns to his Lord in fear and hope – He not only forgives the sin, but replaces those sins for good deeds to the servant's credit. This is from Allah's infinite grace and munificence. Allah says: "Unless he repents, believes, and works righteous deeds, for Allah will change the evil of such persons into good, and Allah is Oft-Forgiving, Most Merciful," [25:70]

إِلَّا مَن تَابَ وَءَامَنَ وَعَمِلَ عَمَلًا صَـٰلِحًا فَأُوْلَـٰٓئِكَ يُبَدِّلُ ٱللَّهُ سَيِّـَٔاتِهِمْ حَسَنَـٰتٍۗ وَكَانَ ٱللَّهُ غَفُورًا رَّحِيمًا ﴿٧٠﴾

Allah says this right after mentioning the sins of polytheism, murder, and adultery. However, this blessing is only for one who has faith, whose repentance is sincere, and who strives to work righteous deeds. Allah's generosity is so far-reaching, that we are not only forgiven through our specific repentance for each sin that we commit, but we can attain forgiveness simply through our constant appeals to Allah to forgive us.

Another way that we attain Allah's forgiveness is through the performance of good deeds. Allah says: "Establish worship at the two ends of the day and in some watches of the night. Lo! Good deeds annul evil deeds. This is reminder for the mindful." [11:114]

وَأَقِمِ ٱلصَّلَوٰةَ طَرَفِ ٱلنَّهَارِ وَزُلَفًا مِّنَ ٱلَّيْلِ إِنَّ ٱلْحَسَنَتِ يُذْهِبْنَ ٱلسَّيِّءَاتِ ذَٰلِكَ ذِكْرَىٰ لِلذَّٰكِرِينَ ﴿١١٤﴾

Some scholars are of the view that his verse is only speaking about the forgiveness of minor sins, and that major sins need specific repentance. They cite the following verse in support of this interpretation: "If you shun the most heinous sins which you are forbidden, We will do away with your small sins and admit you to a gate of great honor." [4:31]

إِن تَجْتَنِبُوا۟ كَبَآئِرَ مَا تُنْهَوْنَ عَنْهُ نُكَفِّرْ عَنكُمْ سَيِّءَاتِكُمْ وَنُدْخِلْكُم مُّدْخَلًا كَرِيمًا ﴿٣١﴾

They also cite a number of hadîth, including the hadîth related by Uthman that the Prophet, peace be upon him, said:

"Any Muslim who offers the prescribed prayer, doing justice to its motions and to the humility that it requires, it will expiate for the sins that preceded it, as long as the person did not commit a major sin." [Sahîh Muslim]

However, Ibn Taymiyah and a number of other scholars consider the verse "Good deeds annul evil deeds" to be general in meaning. It applies to all sins, major and minor. Even if a person's good deeds do not expiate for the sin directly, there can be no doubt that those good deeds weigh in the balance of deeds on the Day of Judgment in a person's favor. Whoever has his good deeds outweigh his evil deeds on that Day will attain salvation.

Allah says: "The balance that day will be true: those whose scale (of good) will be heavy will prosper, and as for those whose measure (of good deeds) is light, their souls will be in perdition, for that they wrongfully treated Our signs." [7:8-9]

وَٱلۡوَزۡنُ يَوۡمَئِذٍ ٱلۡحَقُّ فَمَن ثَقُلَتۡ مَوَٰزِينُهُۥ فَأُوْلَٰٓئِكَ هُمُ ٱلۡمُفۡلِحُونَ ٨

وَمَنۡ خَفَّتۡ مَوَٰزِينُهُۥ فَأُوْلَٰٓئِكَ ٱلَّذِينَ خَسِرُوٓاْ أَنفُسَهُم بِمَا كَانُواْ بِـَٔايَٰتِنَا يَظۡلِمُونَ ٩

Ibn Masûd said: "People will be take into account on the Day of Judgment. Whoever has a single sin to his account more than his good deeds will enter the Fire. Whoever has a single good deed to his account greater than his sinful deeds will enter Paradise."

Then Ibn Mas`ûd recited Allah's words: "...those whose scale (of good) will be heavy, will prosper".

Then he said: "Indeed, the balance will weigh an atom's weight one way or another."

Allah also forgives us our sins through the difficulties that we face in life.

When we are stricken with illness or suffer from circumstances, we will earn forgiveness if we bear them patiently seeking Allah's reward.

Allah forgives our sins on account of the supplications that others make to Allah asking for our forgiveness, including our funeral prayers. We earn forgiveness through the charity we gave in our lives that continue to provide benefit to others after our deaths. We earn forgiveness if we have pious children who beseech Allah on our behalf.

A Muslim's sins are likewise forgiven through the punishment he may receive in the grave. Sins are also forgiven by the intercession that the Prophet, peace be upon him, will make on that day, and then by the intercession of those who are granted intercession. The Prophet, peace be upon him, said: "My intercession is for those who committed major sins from among my followers."

Above and beyond all of this is the mercy of the Most-Merciful Lord who pardons on that Day all sins as He pleases, as long as the person meets Him worshipping Him alone without ascribing to Him any partner.

A Co-wife (the other wife)

Whoever mocks her sister or brother for a sin they repented from will not die till she herself falls into the same sin. Under Islamic marital jurisprudence, a man can take up another wife, but he must treats them all equally. Polygyny (a man marrying up to four wives) is allowed in Islam because there are some circumstances in human history when it is necessary, so it is permissible with conditions as Islam is suitable for all times and places. It is not an unearned male privilege. It is not a means for men to gain pleasure at the expense of women. It is a great responsibility for which a man will be strictly held accountable on the Day of Judgment. While it is true that Islam permits polygyny, it does not require or impose it: marriage can only occur by mutual consent, and a bride can stipulate that her husband-to-be not take a second wife. Likewise, since a bride's consent to marriage is required in Islam, a woman cannot be forced to accept the proposal of a married man.

Monogamy is by far the norm in Muslim societies, as most men cannot afford to maintain more than one family, and many of those who can would rather do without the trouble. However, there are circumstances where the wife would accept the coming of a second wife, as it may be preferable to the available alternatives, and in some cases first wife may actually welcome it. Likewise the new wife may decide that she would rather share the man that she loves than not to be with him at all. There may also be cases where the first wife is ill and is unable to have children. In such circumstances, the second wife, may in fact be the preserver and savior of the marriage and the family.

Everything depends on the attitude of the women themselves, and of course this also depends on the ability of the man to be fair and just always between his wives and the children. Allāh (swt) has made it clear that the man who is not capable and able of doing justice must then only marry one woman.

"And if you fear that you will not deal justly with the orphan girls, then marry those that please you of [other] women, two or three or four. But if you fear that you will not be just, then [marry only] one or those your right hand possesses. That is more suitable that you may not incline [to injustice]. (4:3)

وَإِنْ خِفْتُمْ أَلَّا تُقْسِطُوا فِي الْيَتَمَى فَانكِحُوا مَا طَابَ لَكُم مِّنَ النِّسَاءِ مَثْنَى وَثُلَثَ وَرُبَعَ فَإِنْ خِفْتُمْ أَلَّا تَعْدِلُوا فَوَاحِدَةً أَوْ مَا مَلَكَتْ أَيْمَنُكُمْ ذَلِكَ أَدْنَى أَلَّا تَعُولُوا ۝

The Messenger of Allāh, peace bet upon him, also said that a man with more than one wife, who is not just and fair between them, Allāh will raise him from the grave on the Day of Judgment with half of his limbs hanging off. The "just and fair" towards wives includes the ability to provide for them equally, but not only in material terms, but also to give each wife a fair share of his attention and time, which must include marital (sexual) rights.

The husband must also give each of his wives separate homes or quarters, as was the Sunnah of the Messenger of Allāh, peace and blessings be upon him. If the husband is doing his best to act justly towards all his wives, how should the ideal wife behave to make her family happy? The wife should regard the new wife not as a rival but as a friend and a sister. She should be sympathetic, and must try to exercise self-control, understanding and try to avoid deliberate offences. If she takes the lead in trying to make the new wife happy it will be a great start towards developing friendship and a relationship of kindness between wives. The new wife must try to understand the fears of the first wife. For example, the fear of no longer being the queen of the household, the fear of being ignored or displaced. Such fears, and possible envy if the new wife is more beautiful and younger, are natural human behavior and reactions, and can be calmed if the new wife is kind and uses her initiative to soothe them.

The wives should try to be helpful to one another, and cooperating in the smooth running of the households. If one wife is ill, the other should try to help as much as possible. If one travels or has a job, the other should look after the children. Try to exchange of gifts from often to sustain a kindly relationship. A wife must also be kind to her co-wife's children and to treat them like her own children. She must encourage her own children to be best friends with their half-brothers and sisters. Moreover, a wife must never try to poison her husband's mind against her co-wife or her children. If there is any friction between the wives, they must try to resolve the matter as sisters do. If the man is fair and understanding, a polygamous marriage can be a happy life for all those involved, which has many advantages over the alternative options of divorce or unlawful sexual relationship outside marriage. "And those who say, "Our Lord, grant us from among our wives and offspring comfort to our eyes and make us an example for the righteous." (25:74)

وَٱلَّذِينَ يَقُولُونَ رَبَّنَا هَبْ لَنَا مِنْ أَزْوَٰجِنَا وَذُرِّيَّـٰتِنَا قُرَّةَ أَعْيُنٍ وَٱجْعَلْنَا لِلْمُتَّقِينَ إِمَامًا ﴿٧٤﴾

"O Prophet, say to your wives, "If you should desire the worldly life and its adornment, then come, I will provide for you and give you a gracious release." (33:28)

يَـٰٓأَيُّهَا ٱلنَّبِيُّ قُل لِّأَزْوَٰجِكَ إِن كُنتُنَّ تُرِدْنَ ٱلْحَيَوٰةَ ٱلدُّنْيَا وَزِينَتَهَا فَتَعَالَيْنَ أُمَتِّعْكُنَّ وَأُسَرِّحْكُنَّ سَرَاحًا جَمِيلًا ﴿٢٨﴾

The great responsibility, and trial, of marrying additional wives was emphasized again in the same chapter, stating that it is impossible for a man in his heart to love two or more wives equally. Allah said: You will never be able to be just between your wives, even if it is your ardent desire. Do not incline to one of them and leave the other neglected. If you are righteous and fear Allah, then Allah is ever forgiving and merciful. (4:129)

وَلَن تَسْتَطِيعُوٓا۟ أَن تَعْدِلُوا۟ بَيْنَ ٱلنِّسَآءِ وَلَوْ حَرَصْتُمْ فَلَا تَمِيلُوا۟ كُلَّ ٱلْمَيْلِ فَتَذَرُوهَا كَٱلْمُعَلَّقَةِ وَإِن تُصْلِحُوا۟ وَتَتَّقُوا۟ فَإِنَّ ٱللَّهَ كَانَ غَفُورًا رَّحِيمًا ﴿١٢٩﴾

Scholars derived from these two verses that it is recommended (mustahab) for a man to marry only one wife at a time. An-Nawawi comments on these verses, writing: "It is said in explanation of the verse that you may not wrong them in their rights. It is forbidden to marry more than four wives and it is recommended to be limited to one wife out of fear of wronging them or failing to be just." Source: al-Muhadhab 16:144

Believing men, who sincerely fear Allah, understand the gravity of the situation and would be hesitant to take another wife without a good reason for doing so. In the Hereafter, a man who was unjust between his co-wives will be resurrected with ugly features reflecting his grave sin.

Abu Huraira reported: The Messenger of Allah, peace and blessings be upon him, said: "If a man has two wives and he is not just between them, he will come on the Day of Resurrection with one of his sides collapsed." Source: Sunan al-Tirmidhī 1141

That he comes with one of his sides collapsed is a representation of the unbalanced manner in which he treated his co-wives. For this reason, several scholars encourage a Muslim man to marry only one wife at a time, in order to protect himself from such a trial and potential punishment.

Al-Shafi'i, may Allah have mercy on him, said: "I prefer a man to limit himself to one wife, even though it is permissible for him to marry more, due to the saying of Allah Almighty: If you fear you will not be just, then only one. (4:3) Source: al-Shāfi'ī 11:89

Al-Shafi'i recommended that a man limit himself to one wife, even though it is permissible for him to marry more, in order to protect himself from wronging them by inclining more to some of them or being unable to spend equally upon them. Source: al-Kabīr 11:417

And Ibn Qudamah writes: "The preference is to not marry more than one wife, as mentioned in Al-Mujarrad, due to the saying of Allah Almighty: If you fear you will not be just, then only one. (4:3) And due to His saying: You will never be able to be just between your wives, even if it is your ardent desire. (4:129) Source: al-Kabīr 20:24

And Al-Buhuti writes: "It is recommended not to marry more than one wife if he can maintain chastity with her, as it might expose him to what is forbidden." Source: al-Qina 5:9

Moreover, some scholars stipulated that the prophetic tradition (Sunnah) is for a Muslim man to marry one wife and to only marry another wife if there is an obvious need. The Prophet, peace be upon him, himself was only married to Khadijah (ra) until she passed way, after which he took more wives to meet various needs: to pass on prophetic teachings through them, to solidify familial relationships, to care for widows, and so on.

Al-Shirbini writes: "It is the Sunnah not to marry more than one wife without an obvious need." In some contexts, polygyny could be beneficial and this is why it is permissible with conditions. Some societies have a need to maintain replacement fertility rates, or to care for widows, or to bring family lines together through marriage. In these situations, polygyny may even be necessary if it is performed fairly and for a good purpose.

However, not all social and historical contexts are the same. In many situations, polygyny is not recommended if there is no pressing need for it. Scholars have made this point for at least the last seven hundred years. And according to Al-Shafi'i and the rest of the scholars, it is permissible for a free man to marry up to four free women and it is not permissible to marry more than four. It is recommended not to marry more than one wife, especially in these times of ours. Source: al-Badī'ah 2:195

A man must consider the emotional impact that marrying additional wives would have on his first wife and children. The Prophet, peace be upon him, prohibited Ali (ra) from marrying a second wife while his daughter Fatimah (ra) was still alive, because of the emotional harm it might do to her.

Al-Miswar ibn Makhramah reported: I heard the Messenger of Allah, peace and blessings be upon him, say upon the pulpit:

"Verily, the sons of Hisham ibn al-Mughirah have sought my permission to marry their daughters to Ali ibn Abi Talib. I do not give permission, again I do not give permission, and again I do not give permission, unless Ali ibn Abi Talib intends to divorce my daughter and marry their daughters. Verily, she is only a part of me. I am upset by what upsets her, and I am harmed by what harms her." Source: Ṣaḥīḥ al-Bukhārī 4932

Al-Nawawi commented on this tradition, writing: "The Prophet, peace be upon him, prohibited that because of his compassion for Ali and for Fatimah, and secondly because he feared she would be tested with jealousy." Source: Ṣaḥīḥ Muslim 2449

It is all the more significant that the Prophet, peace be upon him, said this upon the pulpit and not in private, to make it abundantly clear to men that they may not marry a second wife if it harms their first wife. Hence, Ali did not marry additional wives until after Fatimah passed away.

Some impious Muslim men distort the rules and ethics of polygyny in a way that is callous, insensitive, and abusive towards the physical and emotional needs of their wives, as well as their own children and extended families. A man might get bored with his older wife, so he unilaterally decides to marry a second younger wife against his first wife's wishes. A man might also contract a secret second marriage in another country without his first wife and children even knowing about it. These are heinous violations of Islamic teachings.

Thus, the most important character trait in a potential husband is whether or not he fears the punishment of Allah if he is unjust to his wife. Marry your daughter to one who fears Allah. If he loves her, he will honor her. If he hates her, he will not oppress her. The husband's fear of Allah is the first line of protection against marital abuse and domestic violence. Yet this is a qualitative ethical rule, not a quantitative legal rule.

Fear of Allah cannot be accurately tested or measured; a man who fears Allah today may not fear Him tomorrow. So, admonishing men to fear Allah is not a sufficient criterion by itself to protect women. Fortunately, all praise is due to Allah, Islam has a solution to this problem, which provides women with an additional layer of legal protection from abusive husbands who do not fear Allah. A wife has the right to stipulate conditions in the marriage contract that protect her from commonly reported abusive practices.

Uqbah ibn Amr reported: The Messenger of Allah, peace and blessings be upon him, said: "The most worthy of conditions to fulfill in marriage are those that permit intimacy."

And Omar, may Allah be pleased with him, said: "Verily, rights are at the intersection of conditions. You will have what you accepted as conditions."

In other words, men only have rights over their wives in so far as they fulfill the conditions of the marriage contract. Marriage is a reciprocal relationship of love and mercy; it is not based upon men dominating their wives or treating them like disposable commodities. If men violate the terms of their marriage contract, the marriage can be annulled.

Abdur Rahman ibn Ghanm reported: I was sitting closely with Omar ibn al-Khattab, may Allah be pleased with him. A man said: "O commander of the faithful, I married this woman and I accepted her condition that she would keep her house. I have settled my affairs such that I am moving residence to a new land." Omar said, "She has her condition." The man said, "She has ruined men! No woman wishes to divorce her husband but that she may do so?" Omar said: "The Muslims adhere to their conditions at the intersection of their rights."

It is permissible for women and their family guardians to stipulate condition in the marriage contract that the husband may not marry a second wife against her will. If he does so, either in public or secret, she has the right to divorce him. When he marries her and accepts her conditions that she would not be taken out of her house or her country, then she is entitled to her condition. If he marries her and accepts her condition that he will not marry another wife against her will, then she is entitled to separate from him if he marries another wife.

If he accepts her conditions that she will not be taken out of her house or her country, or he will not travel with her, or he will not marry another wife against her will, or he will not take a concubine against her will, these conditions must be fulfilled. If he does not do so, the marriage is annulled. This has been narrated from Omar ibn Al-Khattab, Sa'd ibn Abi Waqqas, Mu'awiyah, and Amr ibn Al-'As, may Allah be pleased with them. It was said by Shuraih, Umar ibn Abdul Aziz, Jabir ibn Zayd, Tawus, Al-Awza'i, and Ishaq.

And Ibn Taymiyyah writes: "When he accepts the condition in the marriage contract that he will not marry another wife against her will, if he marries another wife, the matter is in her hands. This condition is valid and required in the school of Malik, Ahmad, and others. Whenever he marries another wife against her will, the matter is in her hands. If she wishes, she can accept it, and if she wishes, she may separate from him. Allah knows best. Source: al-Fatāwà 32:170

A woman also has the right to divorce her husband if he is physically or emotionally abusive towards her, whether by beating her, burdening her, or neglecting her. Yahya ibn Sa'id reported: Habibah bint Sahl was the wife of Thabit ibn Qays and it was mentioned to the Messenger of Allah, peace and blessings be upon him, that they were married and she was his neighbor. Thabit had struck her, so she appeared at the door of the Messenger of Allah and she said: "Thabit and I can no longer be married."

The Prophet said to Thabit: "Take what she owes to you and let her go her way." Source: Sahih. Lastly, it is not enough for a Muslim man to follow the very minimum legal obligations towards his wives while otherwise committing ethical violations against them. He must also follow Islamic manners and behave with honorable chivalry towards all of the women in his life. Abu Huraira reported: The Messenger of Allah, peace and blessings be upon him, said: The most complete of believers in faith are those with the best character, and the best of you are the best in behavior to their women.

In summary, polygyny is allowed in Islam with strict conditions, but it is recommended for a man to marry only one wife at a time. Polygyny is only permissible if a man is fair to his co-wives and he does not harm any of them physically or emotionally. As legal protection, a wife has the right to stipulate in the marriage contract that her husband may not marry another wife against her wishes. She may also divorce her husband if he abuses or abandons her.

The Unreasonable Husband

Some women are very unfortunate. Their men fail to follow the Prophet's Sunnah. Instead their husbands indulge in various sins that have very adverse effects on the marriage, on the family, and the children. The wife must try to guide and to advise her husband tactfully but very firmly, not by nagging or fighting but in a peaceful heart-to-heart talk. However, if the husband's response is negative or aggressive, she must seek the help of relatives. If that is not possible, then his friends, or a respected Imam (religious scholar) in persuading him to fear Allāh, and to behave in a responsible manner. If this fails, then she it is best to take this matter to a Shari'ah court. If the husband is found guilty of offences that violate the requirements of marriage, the wife must be granted a divorce by the court.

Whoever prefers Allah to all others, Allah will prefer him to others. If a woman fears from her husband contempt or evasion, there is no sin upon them if they make terms of settlement between them - and settlement is best. And present in [human] souls is stinginess. But if you do good and fear Allāh - then indeed Allāh is ever, with what you do, Acquainted. (4:128)

وَإِنِ ٱمۡرَأَةٌ خَافَتۡ مِنۢ بَعۡلِهَا نُشُوزًا أَوۡ إِعۡرَاضًا فَلَا جُنَاحَ عَلَيۡهِمَآ أَن يُصۡلِحَا بَيۡنَهُمَا صُلۡحࣰاۚ وَٱلصُّلۡحُ خَيۡرٌۗ وَأُحۡضِرَتِ ٱلۡأَنفُسُ ٱلشُّحَّۚ وَإِن تُحۡسِنُواْ وَتَتَّقُواْ فَإِنَّ ٱللَّهَ كَانَ بِمَا تَعۡمَلُونَ خَبِيرࣰا ﴿١٢٨﴾

And give women their dowries as a free gift, but if they of themselves be pleased to give up to you a portion of it, then eat it with enjoyment and with wholesome result. (4:4)

وَءَاتُواْ ٱلنِّسَآءَ صَدُقَٰتِهِنَّ نِحۡلَةࣰۚ فَإِن طِبۡنَ لَكُمۡ عَن شَيۡءࣲ مِّنۡهُ نَفۡسࣰا فَكُلُوهُ هَنِيٓـًٔا مَّرِيٓـًٔا ﴿٤﴾

If the wife does not have enough legal help, or evidence, a witness, of her husband's behavior, then she should decide to request for Khul (a divorce by mutual agreement with the husband on the return of the dowry).

Allāh, the Merciful says in the Quran: "And if he has divorced her [for the third time], then she is not lawful to him afterward until [after] she marries a husband other than him. And if the latter husband divorces her [or dies], there is no blame upon the woman and her former husband for returning to each other if they think that they can keep [within] the limits of Allāh . These are the limits of Allāh, which He makes clear to a people who know."

فَإِن طَلَّقَهَا فَلَا تَحِلُّ لَهُۥ مِنۢ بَعۡدُ حَتَّىٰ تَنكِحَ زَوۡجًا غَيۡرَهُۥ ۗ فَإِن طَلَّقَهَا فَلَا جُنَاحَ عَلَيۡهِمَآ أَن يَتَرَاجَعَآ إِن ظَنَّآ أَن يُقِيمَا حُدُودَ ٱللَّهِ ۗ وَتِلۡكَ حُدُودُ ٱللَّهِ يُبَيِّنُهَا لِقَوۡمٍ يَعۡلَمُونَ ﴿٢٣٠﴾

Divorce is very disliked in Islam, and the Prophet, peace and blessings be upon him, warned us against it: "The tasters-male and female," i.e. those who repeatedly marry and divorce exchanging one partner after another." Peace be upon him also said: "Of all the things Allāh (swt) has made lawful, what Allāh most hates is divorce."

The Prophet (peace be upon him) said: "If a wife asks her husband for a divorce without a strong reason for it, the scent of paradise will be forbidden to her forever."

Nonetheless divorce is still available in the final if a marriage is very harmful to the wife, and there is happiness or peace of mind to either of them. If the wife for some reason does not want to divorce her husband in spite of his sins and misbehavior, she must be careful to avoid becoming his accomplice in his sins and evil-doings.

Allāh, the Merciful, said: "Men are the protectors and maintainers of women. Righteous women are devoutly obedient (to Allāh and to their husbands), and guard in the husband's absence what Allāh orders them to guard (e.g. their chastity, their husband's property, etc.). As to those women on whose part you see ill-conduct, admonish them (first), (next), refuse to share their beds, (and last) beat them (lightly, if it is useful), but if they return to obedience, seek not against them means (of annoyance). Surely, Allāh is Ever Most High, Most Great." (4:34)

ٱلرِّجَالُ قَوَّٰمُونَ عَلَى ٱلنِّسَآءِ بِمَا فَضَّلَ ٱللَّهُ بَعْضَهُمْ عَلَىٰ بَعْضٍ وَبِمَآ أَنفَقُواْ مِنْ أَمْوَٰلِهِمْ فَٱلصَّٰلِحَٰتُ قَٰنِتَٰتٌ حَٰفِظَٰتٌ لِّلْغَيْبِ بِمَا حَفِظَ ٱللَّهُ وَٱلَّٰتِى تَخَافُونَ نُشُوزَهُنَّ فَعِظُوهُنَّ وَٱهْجُرُوهُنَّ فِى ٱلْمَضَاجِعِ وَٱضْرِبُوهُنَّ فَإِنْ أَطَعْنَكُمْ فَلَا تَبْغُواْ عَلَيْهِنَّ سَبِيلًا إِنَّ ٱللَّهَ كَانَ عَلِيًّا كَبِيرًا ﴿٣٤﴾

"O you who have believed, obey Allāh and His Messenger and do not turn from him while you hear [his order]." (8:20)

يَـٰٓأَيُّهَا ٱلَّذِينَ ءَامَنُوٓاْ أَطِيعُواْ ٱللَّهَ وَرَسُولَهُۥ وَلَا تَوَلَّوْاْ عَنْهُ وَأَنتُمْ تَسْمَعُونَ ﴿٢٠﴾

"And obey Allāh and His Messenger, and do not dispute and [thus] lose courage and [then] your strength would depart; and be patient. Indeed, Allāh is with the patient." (8:46)

وَأَطِيعُواْ ٱللَّهَ وَرَسُولَهُۥ وَلَا تَنَـٰزَعُواْ فَتَفْشَلُواْ وَتَذْهَبَ رِيحُكُمْ وَٱصْبِرُوٓاْ إِنَّ ٱللَّهَ مَعَ ٱلصَّـٰبِرِينَ ﴿٤٦﴾

This means that everyone is responsible for their own actions, and cannot push off the blame for their own sins on another person or their husband. If the husband is for example a drunkard, then she must never join in his drinking or buy him or serve him beer etc., even if he threatens her or orders her to do it. This is in accordance to the Messenger of Allāh, peace be upon him.

There must never be obedience to a created being in disobedience to the Creator, Allāh (swt). If your husband tries to force you to join him in wrong doing you should ask for a divorce, and a Shari'ah judges are bound under such circumstances to approve the divorce. This follows the same rules as the duty of Hijrah (Migration) for a Muslim if she or he is prohibited from practicing the essentials (pillars) of Islam. Anyone who decides to stay in a place where they are likely to lose their faith and become a part of a corrupt group will be asked by Allāh (swt) on the Day of Judgment why they did not migrate to a land where they would have been able to practice their faith.

"Indeed, those whom the angels take in death while wronging themselves - [the angels] will say, "In what [condition] were you?" They will say, "We were oppressed in the land." The angels will say, "Was not the earth of Allāh spacious [enough] for you to emigrate therein?" For those, their refuge is Hell - and evil it is as a destination." (4:97)

إِنَّ ٱلَّذِينَ تَوَفَّىٰهُمُ ٱلۡمَلَـٰٓئِكَةُ ظَالِمِىٓ أَنفُسِهِمۡ قَالُواْ فِيمَ كُنتُمۡ قَالُواْ كُنَّا مُسۡتَضۡعَفِينَ فِى ٱلۡأَرۡضِۚ قَالُوٓاْ أَلَمۡ تَكُنۡ أَرۡضُ ٱللَّهِ وَٰسِعَةً فَتُهَاجِرُواْ فِيهَاۚ فَأُوْلَـٰٓئِكَ مَأۡوَىٰهُمۡ جَهَنَّمُۖ وَسَآءَتۡ مَصِيرًا ۝

In the same way the faithful wife who has an un-Islamic husband should: must abstain from following and supporting his wrongdoing, must advise him about his behavior, and should seek divorce if the only alternative is to be pulled into sin. An example of one such woman is Asiya bint Muzahim who attained perfect faith as described by the Prophet, peace and blessing be upon him. Asiya lived in ancient Egypt during the rule of the most oppressive pharaoh in history. Not only did she live under his rule, but she lived in his home as his wife. The pharaoh was a horrible tyrant who claimed to be an all-powerful god, and he made his people worship him. At the same time, however, he was so paranoid of being overthrown that he ordered baby boys born in the land to be killed.

In one particular year, the newborn boys could live, and in the next, the newborn boys were killed. It was against this backdrop that Prophet Moses, peace be upon him, was born, in a year the baby boys were to be killed. Asiya loved Moses as her own son. When he started preaching the message of the one true God, she believed wholeheartedly. However, being the wife of the violent and oppressive man who thought himself to be a god, she kept her faith secret. Many men reached perfection but none among the women reached perfection except Mary, the daughter of Imran, the mother of Isa (Jesus) (peace be upon him), and Asiya, Pharaoh's wife. And the superiority of Aisha to other women is like the superiority of Tharid to other kinds of food. According to Hadith, Asiya will be among the first women to enter Paradise. Allāh mentions Asiya as an example to all Muslims. And Allāh presents an example of those who believed: the wife of Pharaoh, when she said: "My Lord, build for me near You a house in Paradise and save me from Pharaoh and his deeds and save me from the wrongdoing people. (66:11)

وَضَرَبَ ٱللَّهُ مَثَلًا لِّلَّذِينَ ءَامَنُواْ ٱمْرَأَتَ فِرْعَوْنَ إِذْ قَالَتْ
رَبِّ ٱبْنِ لِي عِندَكَ بَيْتًا فِي ٱلْجَنَّةِ وَنَجِّنِي مِن فِرْعَوْنَ وَعَمَلِهِ وَنَجِّنِي
مِنَ ٱلْقَوْمِ ٱلظَّٰلِمِينَ ﴿١١﴾

If the wife is not able to get a divorce or cannot break free from the bad husband, then she should take comfort from the Quran verse which says:

Allāh does not charge a soul except [with that within] its capacity. It will have [the consequence of] what [good] it has gained, and it will bear [the consequence of] what [evil] it has earned. Our Lord, do not impose blame upon us if we have forgotten or erred. Our Lord, and lay not upon us a burden like that which You laid upon those before us. Our Lord, and burden us not with that which we have no ability to bear. And pardon us; and forgive us; and have mercy upon us. You are our protector, so give us victory over the disbelieving people. (2:286)

لَا يُكَلِّفُ ٱللَّهُ نَفْسًا إِلَّا وُسْعَهَا لَهَا مَاكَسَبَتْ وَعَلَيْهَا مَا
ٱكْتَسَبَتْ رَبَّنَا لَا تُؤَاخِذْنَآ إِن نَّسِينَآ أَوْ أَخْطَأْنَا رَبَّنَا وَلَا تَحْمِلْ
عَلَيْنَآ إِصْرًا كَمَا حَمَلْتَهُۥ عَلَى ٱلَّذِينَ مِن قَبْلِنَا رَبَّنَا وَلَا تُحَمِّلْنَا
مَا لَا طَاقَةَ لَنَا بِهِۦ وَٱعْفُ عَنَّا وَٱغْفِرْ لَنَا وَٱرْحَمْنَآ أَنتَ مَوْلَىٰنَا
فَٱنصُرْنَا عَلَى ٱلْقَوْمِ ٱلْكَٰفِرِينَ ﴿٢٨٦﴾

In her very difficult situation she should avoid
his sins in accordance with another Hadith: "If
any of you sees wrongdoing they must correct
it with their hand, and if that is not possible
they must correct it with their tongue, and if
that is not possible they should hate it within
their heart, and that is the weakest of faith."

Allah has determined the right foundations of
building the happy Muslim family. In such a
family both spouses have rights on each other
and both of them must fulfill those rights.
Some of these rights are during normal
matrimonial life. Others are during separation
and disagreement. Allah Says:

Divorced women remain in waiting for three periods, and it is not lawful for them to conceal what Allah has created in their wombs if they believe in Allah and the Last Day. And their husbands have more right to take them back in this [period] if they want reconciliation. And due to the wives is similar to what is expected of them, according to what is reasonable. But the men have a degree over them [in responsibility and authority]. And Allah is Exalted in Might and Wise. (2:228)

وَٱلْمُطَلَّقَٰتُ يَتَرَبَّصْنَ بِأَنفُسِهِنَّ ثَلَٰثَةَ قُرُوٓءٍ وَلَا يَحِلُّ لَهُنَّ أَن يَكْتُمْنَ مَا خَلَقَ ٱللَّهُ فِىٓ أَرْحَامِهِنَّ إِن كُنَّ يُؤْمِنَّ بِٱللَّهِ وَٱلْيَوْمِ ٱلْءَاخِرِ وَبُعُولَتُهُنَّ أَحَقُّ بِرَدِّهِنَّ فِى ذَٰلِكَ إِنْ أَرَادُوٓا۟ إِصْلَٰحًا وَلَهُنَّ مِثْلُ ٱلَّذِى عَلَيْهِنَّ بِٱلْمَعْرُوفِ وَلِلرِّجَالِ عَلَيْهِنَّ دَرَجَةٌ وَٱللَّهُ عَزِيزٌ حَكِيمٌ ﴿٢٢٨﴾

Divorce is twice. Then, either keep [her] in an acceptable manner or release [her] with good treatment. And it is not lawful for you to take anything of what you have given them unless both fear that they will not be able to keep [within] the limits of Allah.

But if you fear that they will not keep [within] the limits of Allah, then there is no blame upon either of them concerning that by which she ransoms herself. These are the limits of Allah, do not transgress them. And whoever transgresses the limits of Allah - it is those who are the wrongdoers. (2:229)

الطَّلَٰقُ مَرَّتَانِّ فَإِمْسَاكُ بِمَعْرُوفٍ أَوْ تَسْرِيحُ بِإِحْسَٰنٍّ وَلَا يَحِلُّ لَكُمْ أَن تَأْخُذُوا مِمَّا ءَاتَيْتُمُوهُنَّ شَيْئًا إِلَّا أَن يَخَافَا أَلَّا يُقِيمَا حُدُودَ اللَّهِ فَإِنْ خِفْتُمْ أَلَّا يُقِيمَا حُدُودَ اللَّهِ فَلَا جُنَاحَ عَلَيْهِمَا فِيمَا افْتَدَتْ بِهِۦۚ تِلْكَ حُدُودُ اللَّهِ فَلَا تَعْتَدُوهَاۚ وَمَن يَتَعَدَّ حُدُودَ اللَّهِ فَأُوْلَٰئِكَ هُمُ الظَّٰلِمُونَ ﴿٢٢٩﴾

And if you divorce them before you have touched them and you have already specified for them an obligation, then [give] half of what you specified - unless they forego the right or the one in whose hand is the marriage contract foregoes it. And to forego it is nearer to righteousness. And do not forget graciousness between you. Indeed Allah, of whatever you do, is Seeing. (2:237)

وَإِن طَلَّقْتُمُوهُنَّ مِن قَبْلِ أَن تَمَسُّوهُنَّ وَقَدْ فَرَضْتُمْ لَهُنَّ فَرِيضَةً فَنِصْفُ مَا فَرَضْتُمْ إِلَّا أَن يَعْفُونَ أَوْ يَعْفُوَا۟ ٱلَّذِى بِيَدِهِۦ عُقْدَةُ ٱلنِّكَاحِ وَأَن تَعْفُوٓا۟ أَقْرَبُ لِلتَّقْوَىٰ وَلَا تَنسَوُا۟ ٱلْفَضْلَ بَيْنَكُمْ إِنَّ ٱللَّهَ بِمَا تَعْمَلُونَ بَصِيرٌ ﴿٢٣٧﴾

So, if Islam orders the woman to be obedient to her husband, it also commands the man to respect his wife and respect her feelings and not to help Satan get hold of her. It is unlawful for him to stay away from her for a period that could cause her to be tempted. He also must provide her with accommodation and must spend on her living (feeding her, clothing her, etc.). If the husband falls short of fulfilling his duties, then the woman has the right to ask for her rights unless she gives those rights up without being compelled to do so.

On that tough day, the Day of Judgment, every man, woman, husband, and wife will stand alone, and Allāh knows best what is in their heart.

You, your Family, and Allāh

There are no means of attaining faith and certainty except through the Quran. You must understand that there are three parties to any marriage: the husband, the wife, and Allāh, the Creator and Lord of everyone, who is always a witness. Allah repeatedly gives a reminder that He sees and hears everything." "And establish prayer and give zakat, and whatever good you put forward for yourselves - you will find it with Allāh. (2:110)

وَأَقِيمُوا۟ ٱلصَّلَوٰةَ وَءَاتُوا۟ ٱلزَّكَوٰةَ وَمَا نُقَدِّمُوا۟ لِأَنفُسِكُم مِّنْ خَيْرٍ تَجِدُوهُ عِندَ ٱللَّهِ إِنَّ ٱللَّهَ بِمَا تَعْمَلُونَ بَصِيرٌ ﴿١١٠﴾

And do not make [your oath by] Allāh an excuse against being righteous and fearing Allāh and making peace among people. Allāh is Hears and Knows all. (2:224)

وَلَا تَجْعَلُوا۟ ٱللَّهَ عُرْضَةً لِّأَيْمَٰنِكُمْ أَن تَبَرُّوا۟ وَتَتَّقُوا۟ وَتُصْلِحُوا۟ بَيْنَ ٱلنَّاسِ وَٱللَّهُ سَمِيعٌ عَلِيمٌ ﴿٢٢٤﴾

Husband and wife should always help one another to live as good people, in voluntary submission to Allāh (swt), and in obedience to what He has revealed through His Prophets (peace be upon them). The submissiveness of the wife to the husband is only as a recognition of the husband's position as the head of the family, and not in a servile bond, but as a respect to him. Allāh presents an example of those who disbelieved: the wife of Noah and the wife of Lot. They were under two of Our righteous servants but betrayed them, so those prophets did not avail them from Allāh at all, and it was said, "Enter the Fire with those who enter." (66:10)

ضَرَبَ ٱللَّهُ مَثَلًا لِّلَّذِينَ كَفَرُوٓاْ ٱمْرَأَتَ نُوحٍ وَٱمْرَأَتَ لُوطٍ كَانَتَا تَحْتَ عَبْدَيْنِ مِنْ عِبَادِنَا صَٰلِحَيْنِ فَخَانَتَاهُمَا فَلَمْ يُغْنِيَا عَنْهُمَا مِنَ ٱللَّهِ شَيْئًا وَقِيلَ ٱدْخُلَا ٱلنَّارَ مَعَ ٱلدَّٰخِلِينَ ﴿١٠﴾

In the family, the man should be a responsible leader, and his wife should be a responsible follower.

If he is doing wrong she should tell him, and if she is doing wrong, he should tell her. Both must respond by trying to avoid repeating it. The Prophet, peace and blessing be upon him, said: "Paradise is the reward for a woman who pleases her husband until death."

A wife should try to avoid any behavior that is harmful to her family's welfare in this world or the hereafter, indirectly or directly. Allāh (swt) warns: "O you who have believed, indeed, among your wives and your children are enemies to you, so beware of them. But if you pardon and overlook and forgive - then indeed, Allāh is Forgiving and Merciful." (64:14)

يَٰٓأَيُّهَا ٱلَّذِينَ ءَامَنُوٓا۟ إِنَّ مِنْ أَزْوَٰجِكُمْ وَأَوْلَٰدِكُمْ عَدُوًّا لَّكُمْ فَٱحْذَرُوهُمْ ۚ وَإِن تَعْفُوا۟ وَتَصْفَحُوا۟ وَتَغْفِرُوا۟ فَإِنَّ ٱللَّهَ غَفُورٌ رَّحِيمٌ ۝

The wife should try to be an asset to her family and never a liability. She should encourage everyone in doing good and discourage them from doing wrong.

She must never enter marriage with the intention of hunting for what she can get out of it in terms of money and material benefits. A good wife will find happiness and peace of mind corresponding to the devotion and commitment she puts into the marriage. To feel that her own family values and needs her is the true measure of success. A person is urged to be very merciful and forgiving towards others, as she or he hopes for Allāh's forgiveness and mercy on the Last Day.

A wife should therefore forgive any wrongs that were done in the past, and must not continue to rake up old grievances. "Kind words and forgiving of faults are better than Sadaqah (charity) followed by injury. And Allāh is Rich (Free of all wants) and He is Most-Forbearing." (2:263)

۞ قَوْلٌ مَّعْرُوفٌ وَمَغْفِرَةٌ خَيْرٌ مِّن صَدَقَةٍ يَتْبَعُهَآ أَذًى ۗ وَٱللَّهُ غَنِيٌّ حَلِيمٌ ۝

The family must try to find time always to read the Quran and Hadith together. This will help them to understand the laws of Allāh and to live by them in their daily life, thereby increasing their faith. Allāh instructs and warns you concerning your children. The mother is always the first school. She must be fair, loving, and affectionate to all her children. She must direct them towards what is good and away from what is unlawful. The Prophet (peace be upon him) said: "Be generous to all your children, and excel in teaching them the best of manners and conduct." Ibn Umar reported the Prophet (peace be upon him) said: "What does a mother and father leave as an inheritance for their sons and daughters (that is) better than good morals?"

As the children grow up, both mother and father must teach and demonstrate Islam by example. Children also love stories and can benefit from those which have a moral message. Read to them *Stories of the Prophets*. Teach them about the last Prophet, peace be upon him.

Teach them about Prophet Noah (Nuh), peace be upon him, and Islam. Tell them about the ark that saved Noah and his family from the flood. If it is prayer time the mother and father should call their children to pray. After prayer, the parents can spend a few minutes explaining the Quranic verses so that the children over the years grow up with a broad knowledge of the teachings of Islam. As the children grow bigger the discussions can be extended further by reading from the *Quran, Hadith, Seerah of Prophet Muhammad* (biography of the Prophet, peace be upon him) and many other books that encourages the young child to realize Islam as the guiding force in his or her life. "Our Lord, and send among them a messenger from themselves who will recite to them Your verses and teach them the Book and wisdom and purify them. Indeed, You are the Exalted in Might, the Wise." (2:129)

رَبَّنَا وَٱبْعَثْ فِيهِمْ رَسُولًا مِّنْهُمْ يَتْلُواْ عَلَيْهِمْ ءَايَـٰتِكَ وَيُعَلِّمُهُمُ ٱلْكِتَـٰبَ وَٱلْحِكْمَةَ وَيُزَكِّيهِمْ إِنَّكَ أَنتَ ٱلْعَزِيزُ ٱلْحَكِيمُ ﴿١٢٩﴾

You are that messenger to your children. In this way your children inshaAllāh (if God wills) will grow up and become a source of comfort and joy to the parents. The Messenger of Allāh (peace be upon him) said that leaving behind good and righteous sons and daughters who will pray for their parents is a Sadaqatun Jariatan (continuous charity) that will bring great blessings to the parents even after their death.

This is the religion of the Messenger of Allāh (peace and blessings be upon him). Islam teaches good will and compassion to all creatures. The ideal Muslim woman must never be in competition with her family or husband. Her soul was created by Allāh, so that proves that her soul is her husband's equal. But in any marriage a woman's role is complementary to that of her husband. Her responsibilities and duties are not the same as his. She can fulfil her responsibilities by putting aside her selfish desires and wants. She must understand that her family is always her first priority after her duty to Allāh.

The Messenger of Allāh, peace be upon him, said: "If I had ordered that anyone should prostrate before another, I would have ordered that a wife should prostrate before her husband." But such prostration, submission, to a man would be shirk (associating someone with Allāh (swt) in worship) which is an unforgivable sin.

Nonetheless, the Prophet's words makes it clear the love and commitment a wife must have towards her husband. This is much easier for her to do if her husband is doing his part as being a loving father and husband in accordance with the saying of the Messenger of Allāh, peace be upon him: "the best of you is that who is the kindest to his wife." Allāh has made for you from yourselves mates and has made for you from your mates sons and grandchildren and has provided for you from the good things. Then in falsehood do they believe and in the favor of Allāh they disbelieve? (16:72).

وَٱللَّهُ جَعَلَ لَكُم مِّنْ أَنفُسِكُمْ أَزْوَٰجًا وَجَعَلَ لَكُم مِّنْ أَزْوَٰجِكُم بَنِينَ وَحَفَدَةً وَرَزَقَكُم مِّنَ ٱلطَّيِّبَٰتِ أَفَبِٱلْبَٰطِلِ يُؤْمِنُونَ وَبِنِعْمَتِ ٱللَّهِ هُمْ يَكْفُرُونَ ﴿٧٢﴾

Be kind to your husband always. But if you cooperate against him—then indeed Allah is his protector. Perhaps his Lord, if he divorced you [all], would substitute for him wives better than you - submitting [to Allah], believing, devoutly obedient, repentant, worshipping, and traveling - [ones] previously married and virgins. (66:5)

عَسَىٰ رَبُّهُۥٓ إِن طَلَّقَكُنَّ أَن يُبْدِلَهُۥٓ أَزْوَٰجًا خَيْرًا مِّنكُنَّ مُسْلِمَٰتٍ مُّؤْمِنَٰتٍ قَٰنِتَٰتٍ تَٰٓئِبَٰتٍ عَٰبِدَٰتٍ سَٰٓئِحَٰتٍ ثَيِّبَٰتٍ وَأَبْكَارًا ﴿٥﴾

Do not marry Al-Mushrikat (idolatresses, etc.) till they believe (worship Allah Alone). And indeed a slave woman who believes is better than a (free) Mushrikah (idolatress, etc.), even though she pleases you. And give not (your daughters) in marriage to Al-Mushrikun till they believe (in Allah Alone) and verily, a believing slave is better than a (free) Mushrik (idolater, etc.), even though he pleases you.

Those (Al-Mushrikun) invite you to the Fire, but Allah invites (you) to Paradise and Forgiveness by His Leave, and makes His Ayat (proofs, evidences, verses, lessons, signs, revelations, etc.) clear to mankind that they may remember. [2:221]

وَلَا تَنكِحُوا ٱلْمُشْرِكَٰتِ حَتَّىٰ يُؤْمِنَّ وَلَأَمَةٌ مُّؤْمِنَةٌ خَيْرٌ مِّن مُّشْرِكَةٍ وَلَوْ أَعْجَبَتْكُمْ وَلَا تُنكِحُوا ٱلْمُشْرِكِينَ حَتَّىٰ يُؤْمِنُوا وَلَعَبْدٌ مُّؤْمِنٌ خَيْرٌ مِّن مُّشْرِكٍ وَلَوْ أَعْجَبَكُمْ أُوْلَٰئِكَ يَدْعُونَ إِلَى ٱلنَّارِ وَٱللَّهُ يَدْعُوٓا۟ إِلَى ٱلْجَنَّةِ وَٱلْمَغْفِرَةِ بِإِذْنِهِۦ وَيُبَيِّنُ ءَايَٰتِهِۦ لِلنَّاسِ لَعَلَّهُمْ يَتَذَكَّرُونَ ﴿٢٢١﴾

Whoever does righteousness, whether male or female, while he is a believer - We will surely cause him to live a good life, and We will surely give them their reward [in the Hereafter] according to the best of what they used to do. (16:97)

مَنْ عَمِلَ صَٰلِحًا مِّن ذَكَرٍ أَوْ أُنثَىٰ وَهُوَ مُؤْمِنٌ فَلَنُحْيِيَنَّهُۥ حَيَوٰةً طَيِّبَةً وَلَنَجْزِيَنَّهُمْ أَجْرَهُم بِأَحْسَنِ مَا كَانُوا۟ يَعْمَلُونَ ﴿٩٧﴾

A person of faith is one who fears the death of his heart, not of his body. A true believer does not fear physical death, rather he fears the death of his heart. Ibn Taymiyah said: "When I am confused in my understanding of anything or an issue in Islam, I forthwith beseech Allah to forgive me one thousand times sometimes a little more or sometimes a little less. Then Allah opens what was closed for me and I come to understand." Ask forgiveness of your Lord, surely He is the most Forgiving." (71:10)

فَقُلْتُ ٱسْتَغْفِرُوا۟ رَبَّكُمْ إِنَّهُۥ كَانَ غَفَّارًا ﴿١٠﴾

Allah will let loose the sky for you in plenteous rain (forgiveness): (71:11)

يُرْسِلِ ٱلسَّمَآءَ عَلَيْكُم مِّدْرَارًا ﴿١١﴾

Always the best way to finding inner peace is to always seek forgiveness from Allah. Even a sin can be a blessing if it causes the believer to turn to his Allah in repentance. Allah does not make a decree for his slave except that it is better for him.

In regards to this hadith, Ibn Taymiyah was asked: "Even the sin?" He replied: "Yes, if it is followed by repentance and regret, asking for forgiveness, and a sincere feeling of remorse for having transgressed."

And We did not send any messenger except to be obeyed by permission of Allah. And if, when they wronged themselves, they had come to you, [O Muhammad], and asked forgiveness of Allah and the Messenger had asked forgiveness for them, they would have found Allah Accepting of repentance and Merciful. (4:64)

وَمَآ أَرْسَلْنَا مِن رَّسُولٍ إِلَّا لِيُطَاعَ بِإِذْنِ اللَّهِ وَلَوْ أَنَّهُمْ إِذ ظَّلَمُوٓاْ أَنفُسَهُمْ جَآءُوكَ فَاسْتَغْفَرُواْ اللَّهَ وَاسْتَغْفَرَ لَهُمُ الرَّسُولُ لَوَجَدُواْ اللَّهَ تَوَّابًا رَّحِيمًا ﴿٦٤﴾

If pain should touch you - there has already touched the [opposing] people a wound similar to it. And these days [of varying conditions] We alternate among the people so that Allah may make evident those who believe and [may] take to Himself from among you martyrs - and Allah does not like the wrongdoers. (3:140)

إِن يَمْسَسْكُمْ قَرْحٌ فَقَدْ مَسَّ الْقَوْمَ قَرْحٌ مِّثْلُهُ وَتِلْكَ الْأَيَّامُ
نُدَاوِلُهَا بَيْنَ النَّاسِ وَلِيَعْلَمَ اللَّهُ الَّذِينَ ءَامَنُوا وَيَتَّخِذَ مِنكُمْ
شُهَدَاءَ وَاللَّهُ لَا يُحِبُّ الظَّالِمِينَ ﴿١٤٠﴾

It will be, on the Day they see it, as though they had not remained [in the world] except for an afternoon or a morning thereof. (79:46)

كَأَنَّهُمْ يَوْمَ يَرَوْنَهَا لَمْ يَلْبَثُوا إِلَّا عَشِيَّةً أَوْ ضُحَىٰهَا ﴿٤٦﴾

Even though the Prophet, peace and blessings be upon him, faced so much difficulties and hardships, His faith never wavered. He was in the cave with Abu Bakr (may Allah be pleased with him), with his enemies near them, and he said to his Companion: "Do not grieve; indeed Allah is with us." And Allah sent down his tranquility upon him and supported him with angels you did not see and made the word of those who disbelieved the lowest, while the word of Allah - that is the highest. And Allah is Exalted in Might and Wise. (9:40)

$$\text{إِلَّا تَنصُرُوهُ فَقَدْ نَصَرَهُ اللَّهُ إِذْ أَخْرَجَهُ الَّذِينَ كَفَرُوا}$$

$$\text{ثَانِيَ اثْنَيْنِ إِذْ هُمَا فِي الْغَارِ إِذْ يَقُولُ لِصَاحِبِهِ لَا}$$

$$\text{تَحْزَنْ إِنَّ اللَّهَ مَعَنَا ۖ فَأَنزَلَ اللَّهُ سَكِينَتَهُ عَلَيْهِ}$$

$$\text{وَأَيَّدَهُ بِجُنُودٍ لَّمْ تَرَوْهَا وَجَعَلَ كَلِمَةَ الَّذِينَ}$$

$$\text{كَفَرُوا السُّفْلَىٰ ۗ وَكَلِمَةُ اللَّهِ هِيَ الْعُلْيَا ۗ وَاللَّهُ}$$

$$\text{عَزِيزٌ حَكِيمٌ ﴿٤٠﴾}$$

Before the battle of Badr, the Prophet, peace and blessings be upon him, eagerly put on his armor while saying: Their will their multitude be put to flight, and they will show their backs. (54:45)

$$\text{سَيُهْزَمُ الْجَمْعُ وَيُوَلُّونَ الدُّبُرَ ﴿٤٥﴾}$$

And in the battle of Uhud, after many of his Companions were murdered and others were injured, the Prophet, peace and blessings be upon him, said to his Companions: "Line up behind me so that I can praise my Lord." It was the determination and will power of a Prophet, peace and blessings be upon him that could even, by the will of Allah, shake mountains.

If someone close to you has died, you probably feel overwhelmed with grief. It is a natural and human response to loss. Qays ibn Aasim al-Manqari, famous among the Arabs for his patience, was once narrating a story to some of his companions, when a man came and told Qays: "Your son has been killed. The son of so-and-so was the culprit." Qays did not cut his story short, but instead continued relating it in a calm demeanor until he finished. Then he said: "Wash my son, shroud him, and allow me to pray over him!" And [those who] are patient in poverty and hardship and during battle. Those are the ones who have been true, and it is those who are the righteous. (2:177)

Ikrimah ibn Abi Jahl (may Allah be pleased with him) was offered water on his deathbed, and he said: "He raised his hands and prayed "Allah, I earnestly seek You." Then said: "please offer the water to so and so." There were a number of them, .all on the verge of dying, and each preferred the person beside him to his own self, and with this wonderful display of courage and brotherhood they all died.

Lastly I ask Allāh (swt) for forgiveness for any mistake I might have made, and pray that it will be acceptable to Him.

The Prophet's Prayer

Peace and Blessings Be Upon Him

اَللّٰهُمَّ اِلَيْكَ اَشْكُوْ ضَعْفَ قُوَّتِيْ وَقِلَّةَ حِيْلَتِيْ وَهَوَانِيْ عَلَى النَّـــــاسِ يَاۤ اَرْحَمَ الرَّاحِمِيْنَ اَنْتَ رَبُّ الْمُسْتَضْعَفِيْنَ وَاَنْتَ رَبِّيْ اِلٰى مَنْ تَكِلُنِيْ اِلٰى بَعِيْدٍ يَّتَجَهَّمُنِيْ اَمْ اِلٰى عَدُوٍّمَّلَّكْتَهُ اَمْرِيْ اِنْ لَّمْ يَكُنْ بِكَ عَلَيَّ غَضَبٌ فَلَاۤ اُبَالِيْ وَلٰكِنَّ عَافِيَتَكَ هِيَ اَوْسَعُ لِيْ اَعُوْذُ بِنُوْرِ وَجْهِكَ الَّذِيْ اَشْرَقَتْ لَهُ الظُّلُمَاتُ وَصَلُحَ عَلَيْهِ اَمْرُ الدُّنْيَـــــــا وَالْاٰخِرَةِ مِنْ اَنْ تُنْزِلَ بِيْ غَضَبَكَ اَوْ يَحِلَّ عَلَيَّ سَخَطَكَ لَكَ الْعُتْبٰى حَتّٰى تَرْضٰى وَلَا حَوْلَ وَلَا قُوَّةَ اِلَّا بِكَ

"O'Allāh, to You do I complain of my weakness, little resource and lowliness before men. O'Most Merciful of those who show mercy, You are the Lord of the weak and You are my Lord. To whom will You leave me? To a far-off stranger who will mistreat me? Or to an enemy to whom You have granted power over me? If You are not angry with me, then I care not, but Your favour is better for me.

I seek refuge in the Light of Your Countenance by which the darkness is illumined and the things of this world and the next are set aright, lest Your anger descend upon me, or Your wrath light upon me. It is You Whom we beseech until You are well pleased. There is no power, and no strength except in You."

Published for Allāh (SWT), not for profit

www.ingramcontent.com/pod-product-compliance
Lightning Source LLC
Chambersburg PA
CBHW050224270326
41914CB00003BA/562